Love, Laughter, and Rhubarb

by Tinky Weisblat

The Merry Lion Press
Hawley, Massachusetts

Love, Laughter, and Rhubarb. Copyright 2018 by Tinky Weisblat. All rights reserved. No part of this book may be reproduced or transmitted in any form or by any means, electronic or mechanical—except by a reviewer who may quote brief passages in a review to be printed in a magazine or newspaper, or on the web—without permission in writing from the publisher.

The Merry Lion Press
84 Middle Road
Hawley, MA 01339

First printing 2018.

Publisher's Cataloging-in-Publication Data

Weisblat, Tinky
Love, Laughter, and Rhubarb
by Tinky Weisblat

ISBN: 13: 978-0-9742741-1-9

Library of Congress Control Number: 2018900050

1. Weisblat, Tinky. 2. Rhubarb. 3. Cooking with rhubarb
4. Rhubarb—use in cooking.
5. Cooking, American—New England Style.

Printed in China.

Table of Contents

Introduction
A Passion for Rhubarb — 5

Beverages and Appetizers
A Little History — 13
Recipes — 16

Sides, Salads, and Breads
Rhubarb and Hope — 27
Recipes — 29

Main Dishes and Condiments
Forcing Rhubarb — 41
Recipes — 43

A Green Digression
Dandelion Greens and Asparagus — 61
Recipes — 63

Pies and Tarts
Rhubarb Country — 69
Recipes — 71

Rhubarb, Rhubarb, Rhubarb!
A Meaningful Word — 81
"Wet" Recipes — 83

Bars and Cakes
Rhubarb in Fiction — 95
Recipes — 98

Odds and Ends
Acknowledgments — 113
A Note About Cooking with Rhubarb/Afterword — 114

— 117

This early postcard from British artist Donald McGill spells rhubarb incorrectly, but it echoes my sentiments about the plant!

Introduction

A Passion for Rhubarb

Rhubarb may not seem like the sort of food that inspires passion. It's an ordinary plant, one found growing in weed-like profusion in many yards in northern climes.

Its flavor is far from subtle. Its texture is far from sensuous. And yet I adore it so much that I am devoting this small tome to the object of my passion.

My sister-in-law Leigh, always a source of good advice, tells me that I am obliged to justify this book to readers.

Like many Americans, Leigh has a low opinion of rhubarb. At one point her family lived in Alaska, where that plant grows with abandon. Leigh's mother Mary served a LOT of rhubarb. Leigh found Mary's rhubarb creations sour and resented being asked to eat them.

Leigh believes that others may feel the same way about rhubarb. She may be right. I admit that even I didn't always love rhubarb. When I was a small child, in fact, I shared Leigh's disdain for it.

My farm-raised mother and grandmother both doted on rhubarb and frequently urged the small Tinky to partake of what they considered a treat. I scorned the idea.

Rhubarb was tart, and I was a lover of sweets. It was oddly stringy, and I favored uniform texture in my food. It was old fashioned, and I prided myself on embracing the new. I eschewed it for years.

One spring afternoon in the 1990s, however, I looked at the rhubarb growing cheerfully in the backyard and made up my mind to stew some and eat it. I'm not sure why I gave rhubarb another try after all those years.

Perhaps it had to do with changing relationships. My grandmother had died, and my mother was aging. Eating a plant they loved suddenly seemed like a tribute to them rather than a surrender.

It may be that I had matured enough to see the value of things that were tart, complex, and old fashioned.

In the years since, rhubarb has become my favorite food. I love its rich color, its adaptability, and its long culinary tradition (just another way of saying "old fashioned"). I love the tartness I once rejected, although I do add a little sugar to just about everything I make with my red stalks.

When I adopted a new kitten six years ago, it didn't take me long to start calling her Rhubarb. Like the food for which she is named, Miss Ruby has a complex personality: tart and assertive, yet appealing.

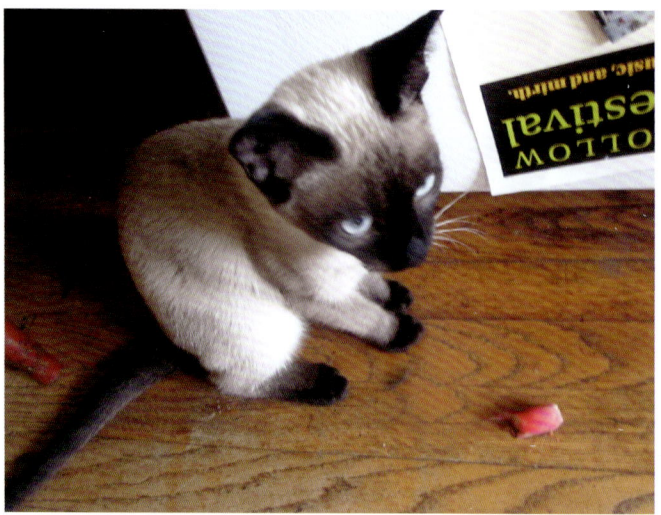

Rhubarb (as a kitten) contemplates rhubarb.

When I began writing a food blog in 2008, I featured rhubarb prominently every spring. I woke up one morning about a year and a half ago and decided to compile those rhubarb recipes into a book. Naturally, I have added many new recipes as well; I love to experiment with rhubarb.

Love, Laughter, and Rhubarb is not meant to be an exhaustive study of rhubarb. Like the rhubarb patch in a rambling New England garden, this book is a small but (I hope) tasty part of an ongoing tradition. It is a stew with a number of ingredients—a bit of history, a few tips for cooking, a number of unusual but also usual recipes.

When in the course of conversation I discover that someone I have met is a fellow rhubarb lover, something special happens. Rhubarb enthusiasts don't have a secret handshake … although perhaps we should invent one. The hands could meet and then retreat from each other at a slight angle, mimicking the gesture one makes when picking rhubarb.

We do share a smile and a glow in our eyes as we admit that we enjoy a food unknown to many.

This book is addressed to anyone with that glow. I hope you'll contact me after you read it to share your tales and recipes of rhubarb.

I also hope that *Love, Laughter, and Rhubarb* will convince a few non-enthusiasts to give rhubarb a chance. After being subjected to my recipe testing, Leigh is actually beginning to like the stuff.

She is a loyal sister-in-law so she understood and tolerated my need to test rhubarb recipes from the start. Nevertheless, she was less than thrilled at the prospect of eating a lot of rhubarb.

I think the turning point as far as Leigh was concerned was tasting rhubarb curd. She looked skeptical when I offered her the first small spoonful. As I point out in its recipe, it's not a prepossessing-looking substance.

Once the curd hit her taste buds, however, Leigh's eyes lit up.

She hasn't enjoyed every rhubarb recipe as much as the curd. She hasn't actively disliked any of my test recipes, however. And one or two have entered her culinary repertoire. The day after I made my "Rhubarb with Cocoa" brownies, she was moved to make another batch herself; the first had disappeared remarkably quickly.

I can't go into the home of every rhubarb skeptic out there and cook with rhubarb in his or her kitchen. I do hope, however, that this book will encourage non-cognoscenti to give rhubarb a try.

Introduction 7

I firmly believe that the object of my passion is due for a food-fashion renaissance.

With a little care (and the right climate—it does like cold weather!), rhubarb will grow happily in your yard, ready to greet you and feed you in the spring. After dandelion greens, it's the first food we can harvest from the ground each year in my hometown of Hawley, Massachusetts.

Rhubarb thus represents not just nourishment and old-fashioned virtues but spring itself.

Join me as I salute and cook with this special plant. You may not end up feeling undying passion for rhubarb—but I predict that you'll respect it just a little more after reading this book! With luck, you'll find recipes that speak to you as the curd and brownies spoke to my sister-in-law.

Before I get to my recipes, you may be wondering why this book is called *Love, Laughter, and Rhubarb*.

Love, laughter, and food (with a special emphasis on rhubarb) are my touchstones.

My last book, *Pulling Taffy*, recalled taking care of my mother in the final year of her life. I learned many things that year—but above all I learned always to have love in my heart: for friends, for family, for neighbors, for our world. Love gives meaning to the most difficult moments we face and also to the most mundane ones. (Sometimes, ironically, the mundane is harder to take than the difficult.)

As for laughter, I can't imagine doing without it. My sense of humor helps me see the upside of any situation. In hard times it alleviates sadness and keeps me from falling into the sort of despond that my dramatic personality would otherwise embrace. Laughter is healthy, physically and psychologically. Like love and food, it helps me connect with those around me. People are drawn to smiles and laughter.

I seriously can't imagine doing without rhubarb, either. Its flavorful red stalks nourish my friends, give me hope (more on that later), and inspire me to get creative in the kitchen.

As I wrote in my previous cookbook, rhubarb is a visible and flavorful reminder of people in my past who shared some of that plant's characteristics: color, straightforwardness, and tenacity. In *The Pudding Hollow Cookbook*, I explored the ways in which rhubarb helps me remember my maternal grandmother and a grandmother-like neighbor I adored. It also reminds me of my late mother Jan (a.k.a. Taffy), who was as full of life and flavor as anyone I have ever known and who pretty much defined the word "stubborn."

Taffy wasn't really going to hit me (I THINK!).

In addition, rhubarb brings back memories of Taffy's favorite aunt. My Great-Aunt Charlotte had a tough life. (I know the correct term is "Grandaunt," but we called her "great." And she was.) After their parents' death when they were small, she and her two sisters, Alma and Clara (my grandmother), lived in an orphanage for several years. Charlotte was eventually adopted by a couple who saw her as a workhorse rather than a daughter.

The wife disliked Charlotte and beat her. Eventually, this "mother" decided she had had enough of the young girl. She took the child out of school at lunchtime one day when Charlotte was only 13 and put her on a train to New York. Charlotte found a series of jobs, worked hard, and ended up marrying a kind but emotionally unstable man who died young and left her with a struggling business and two children. She spent many of her later years taking care of her ailing elder sister, Alma.

Through all this, Aunt Charlotte never complained. Like rhubarb in poor soil, she stood up straight, asserted herself, and endured. She died at 106 a happy woman despite a relatively unhappy life.

My favorite Aunt Charlotte story dates from the 1970s, when she was in her 80s. Walking down the street one day in her slightly dicey New Jersey neighborhood, she came across a gang of teenagers tormenting a smaller boy. Aunt Charlotte positioned herself in front of the victim, assumed a boxing stance, and declared, "Put up your dukes!" in her working-class accent. The teenagers were so astonished by her sheer nerve that they left the boy alone.

I'm not sure I'd have the courage to do something like that—but I'd like to think I would. I spend a lot of my life trying to emulate Aunt Charlotte's wisdom and strength.

I have one more passion I'd like to mention. Music is a mainstay of my life, even if I didn't put it in the title of this book. ("Love, Laughter, Rhubarb, and Music" seemed an awfully wordy title for a volume that in the final analysis isn't very long.) It got me through taking care of my mother, for whom it was a balm and a joy. It gets me through tough days and years.

I sing every day. I'm inspired by my neighbor, the renowned composer and conductor Alice Parker. At 92, Alice is as busy as ever composing, teaching, and leading music lovers in song.

For many years, she and I have enjoyed part-time second careers as the Divas of Hawley, Massachusetts. Alice holds forth at the piano, and I croon American popular standards to anyone who will listen. We always end our performances with a sing-along set. When everyone in a room is singing, magic fills the air.

I hope that some of the love and humor I try to embrace in my life have spilled over into these pages and will bring a little pleasure to my readers as they contemplate rhubarb. I couldn't put music in the book, but I hope you'll sing a song or two as you make the recipes. Welcome to my world and my kitchen.

Beverages and Appetizers

A Little History

> *What rhubarb, cyme, or what purgative drug*
> *Would scour these English hence?*
>
> *Macbeth*

In Shakespeare's day—and for centuries before—rhubarb was known as a medicinal plant, not a food.

The roots of the plant were ground into a powder and used to aid the digestive system, particularly as an astringent (in small doses) or laxative (in larger doses). Unlike many other natural laxatives, it apparently produced few side effects. The title of Clifford Foust's book *Rhubarb: The Wondrous Drug* (Princeton University Press, 1992) stems from rhubarb's popularity as a medicine. Foust writes of the plant's "immense value to society over centuries." In his *Medical Toxicology of Natural Substances* (Wiley, 2008), Donald G. Barceloux calls rhubarb the "All Bran of the Age of Reason."

Rhubarb comes from a variety of countries but is best known as a Chinese import. I once met a woman in western Massachusetts whose grandparents brought rhubarb plants back from a stint as missionaries in China; the descendants of the plants still feed the descendants of the missionaries.

In the past rhubarb enjoyed far more prestige than it does today. In a 2013 *Saveur* article, "Good Stalk: Rhubarb," Dara Moskowitz Grumdahl explains, "In 17th-century Russia, rhubarb was so valuable that much of the country's treasury was derived from the medicinal sales of the imported rhubarb root."

She adds, "When Chinese emperors and Russian czars had a border dispute, withholding rhubarb was China's biggest weapon."

As many would-be rhubarb growers have learned, rhubarb doesn't reproduce well from seed; it is best bred by dividing existing plants. Growing rhubarb thus works well if your neighbor gives you a plant, but it proved difficult for Europeans attempting to transplant it from China. Still, they tried for centuries to grow what Foust calls "that elusive rhubarb."

Eventually they succeeded, more or less. According to Foust, rhubarb gained prominence as a food in Europe only in the 19th century—and the rhubarb used for cooking was a hybrid of different varieties that had been used previously as medicines.

One factor that helped culinary rhubarb achieve popularity in Europe and the United States was the increasing availability and affordability of sugar in that era. Foust notes:

> By the second quarter of the nineteenth century, Caribbean sugar had declined in price so far over the preceding century that its consumption had risen enormously. Although not as cheap and plentiful as it was to become by the end of the century, it was already easily available to the middle and poorer classes of Britain, the continent, and the New World. Sugar in its several forms made possible the widespread use and enjoyment of formerly shunned fruits and vegetables whose sour tastes were too disagreeable for ordinary use, no matter how healthful they may have been. Sugar also contributed to their preservation in glass or tins....

(As you will see from the recipes throughout this book, rhubarb does generally require the addition of a little sweetness to achieve its best flavor.)

Rhubarb's reputation as a medicine kept it from taking the United States by storm for many years. Robert S. Cox reports in *New England Pie* (American Palate, 2015) that a journalistic promoter of American crops known as "Agricola" wrote in the 1820s that the plant's name "in some instances prevented its culinary use … in order to prevent a previous nausea and disgust."

"Fortunately," Cox goes on to explain, "some unnamed proto-PR genius came up with the name 'pie plant' to divert attention." To many Americans, rhubarb still goes by that name—and is primarily used in pie.

The peak of rhubarb production in the United States dated from the early 20th century until the 1940s. Foust goes so far as to call the love of eating rhubarb in Britain and the United States "culinary rhubarb mania." In World War II, he explains, the rationing of sugar and the siphoning of farm laborers to defense work hit rhubarb growers in this country hard. And so American rhubarb cultivation moved mostly into people's backyards, with some large-scale agricultural production remaining in cooler places such as Washington State and Michigan.

Part of me would love to see rhubarb revived as a prestige plant, beloved of both kings and common people. Another part of me is happy to treasure it quietly, to be "in the know" when many people have forgotten this delectable plant. Rhubarb doesn't seem to care. It just keeps pushing its leaves and stalks up in the garden.

It doesn't even care what you call it. Rhubarb is technically a vegetable, but since 1947 it has officially been a fruit in the United States, thanks to the U.S. Customs Court in Buffalo, New York. The court ruled that rhubarb would be deemed a fruit in the United States, since it was generally treated as one, and subject to the lower import tax on fruit. (I have no idea why vegetables are more expensive to import than fruits. I suspect some chicanery on the part of the United Fruit Company.)

Whether you call rhubarb a fruit or a vegetable, I hope you'll enjoy the recipes for beverages and appetizers that follow.

Rhubarb Bitters

I wish I could claim this recipe as my own. In fact, it comes from a terrific book, Bitters, *by Brad Thomas Parsons (Ten Speed Press, 2011). The author kindly gave me permission to use his recipe when I told him that my brother and sister-in-law love Manhattans and prefer these bitters in their cocktails to any commercial brand.*

The ingredients aren't inexpensive or easy to come by. I used a combination of sources: a local health-food store and the online store of Kalustyan's, a specialty-food shop in New York City. The bitters last a long time, however, and make a lovely offering for anyone on your gift list who likes cocktails.

1-1/2 cups fresh rhubarb, chopped
the zest of 1/2 grapefruit, cut into strips with a paring knife
the zest of 1/2 orange, cut into strips with a paring knife
the zest of 1 lime, cut into strips with a paring knife
1/2 teaspoon coriander seeds, cracked
1 teaspoon grains of paradise, cracked
1/2 tablespoon nigella seeds
1/2 teaspoon gentian root
4 dried hibiscus flowers
1/2 teaspoon horehound
1/2 teaspoon sarsaparilla
2 cups high-proof vodka (more if needed)
about 1 cup water
2 tablespoons honey

Place all of the ingredients except the vodka, the water, and the honey in a quart-size Mason jar or other large glass container with a lid. Pour in the 2 cups of vodka, adding more if necessary so that all of the ingredients are covered. Close the jar tightly and store at room temperature out of direct sunlight for 2 weeks, shaking the jar once a day.

After 2 weeks, strain the liquid through a cheesecloth-lined funnel into a clean quart-size jar to remove the solids. Repeat until all of the sediment has been filtered out. Squeeze the cheesecloth over the jar to release any liquids, and transfer the solids to a small nonreactive saucepan. Cover the jar and set it aside.

Cover the solids in the saucepan with water and bring the mixture to a boil over medium-high heat. Cover the saucepan, lower the heat, and simmer for 10 minutes.

Remove the saucepan from the heat and let it cool completely. Once cooled, add the contents of the saucepan (both liquid and solids) to another quart-size Mason jar.

Cover the jar and store it at room temperature out of direct sunlight for 1 week, shaking the jar daily.

After 1 week, strain the jar with the liquids and solids through a cheesecloth-lined funnel into a clean Mason jar. Repeat until all of the sediment has been filtered out. Discard the solids. Add this liquid to the jar containing the original vodka solution.

Add the honey to your mixture, and stir to incorporate; then cover and give the jar a shake to dissolve fully.

Allow the mixture to sit at room temperature for 3 days. At the end of the 3 days skim off any debris that floats to the surface and pour the mixture through a cheesecloth-lined funnel one last time to remove any solids.

Using a funnel, decant the bitters into smaller jars and label them. If there is any sediment left in the bitters, or if the liquid is cloudy, give the bottle a shake before using. The bitters will last indefinitely, but for optimal flavor use them within a year.

Makes about 20 ounces. (I put my bitters into four 5-ounce bottles.)

The Madame Rhubarb

"Madame Rhubarb" is the name I have given to my brother and sister-in-law's favorite tipple, which is basically a Manhattan made with rhubarb bitters. Rhubarb is much more of a Massachusetts flavor than a Manhattan one—and the name "Madame Rhubarb" is steeped in the history of alcohol in my home state. The name originated in the Vernon Hotel in Worcester.

The Vernon housed one of Worcester's best known speakeasies during the Prohibition Era. Worcester was a hard-drinking town. According to food writer Giselle Rivera-Flores, at one time 60 percent of all arrests in this central-Massachusetts city stemmed from public drunkenness.

When the city went dry, not everyone stopped drinking. The Vernon created a speakeasy in its basement. Photos of this dark area of the hotel make it look pretty depressing—but no one was coming for the ambiance. The Vernon had special status among Worcester speakeasies: one of its owners was a state trooper. Not surprisingly, the bar was never raided.

One entered the speakeasy via a secret door. True to all the clichés of Prohibition, one had to know the password to get in. When asked, "Who sent you?" the would-be drinker needed to reply, "Madame Rhubarb." Madame Rhubarb was the nickname of a chambermaid at the hotel, a Polish woman whose name was difficult for New Englanders to pronounce.

I hope she wouldn't have minded our appropriating her name for our cocktail. My sister-in-law Leigh is our family's designated mixologist, and this is her formula. Leigh's most important piece of advice is not to "go cheap" on the rye or the cherries. "The quality matters here," she notes. This recipe may be doubled.

lots of ice cubes
several shakes of rhubarb bitters (see pages 16-17)
a few drops of cherry juice from a jar of maraschino cherries (optional; this makes the drink a little sweeter)
1 ounce sweet vermouth
2 ounces rye
1 maraschino cherry (Leigh prefers Luxardo brand)

Fill a cocktail shaker with ice. Shake the bitters onto the ice, followed by the cherry juice if you want to use it. Pour in the vermouth and the rye.

Stir the contents with a long spoon inside the shaker or swirl them with your hand outside it. Do not shake; just stir or swirl. Continue to stir/swirl for a good minute to let some of the ice melt into your drink. Sometimes Leigh lets the drink sit in the shaker for an extra minute or two to dilute the alcohol a little more. Place the cherry in a cocktail glass, and strain the liquid into the glass. Enjoy your cocktail. Serves 1.

"Baby, It's NOT Cold Outside" Strawberry-Rhubarb Daiquiri

My friend Chef Michael Collins informs me that he was inspired to create this cocktail by my late neighbor Florette, who adored her huge rhubarb patch. Michael first served it under this name in 2010 in honor of the centennial of composer Frank Loesser, who wrote "Baby, It's Cold Outside."

I have tried it three ways—with rum (as described below) at Michael's restaurant (now closed, alas), with a little Grand Marnier at home when I couldn't find rum, and in "virgin" form with pink lemonade for my young friend Audrey. It's refreshing all three ways.

for the base:
6 cups water
1 cup sugar
2 cups chopped rhubarb
2 cups strawberries, cut in half
1/2 lime

for the cocktail:
2 ounces white rum
1 cup cocktail base (see above)
lime juice as needed for rimming
sugar as needed for rimming

Bring the water to a boil in a nonreactive saucepan. Add the sugar and stir. When the sugar has dissolved add the fruit.

Reduce the heat to very low and simmer, uncovered, for 20 minutes, until the fruit breaks down.

Allow the mixture to cool. Remove the half lime (DO NOT FORGET THIS STEP!), and place the liquid in a blender in batches. Blend it; then strain it, first using a stainless-steel strainer (don't try to push the fuzz down through the holes) and then through cheesecloth.

Place it in a jar and keep it refrigerated until it is needed.

To make a cocktail (or two): Place the rum in a cocktail shaker, and add ice. Pour in the cup of cocktail base. Shake.

Spread a little lime juice around the rim of 1 large glass or 2 small glasses, and dip it/them in sugar so that the sugar coats the rim(s). Strain the drink into the glass(es).

The drink recipe serves 1 to 2. The base makes about 6 cups.

Rhubarb Syrup and Lemonade

The deep pink syrup can be added to cocktails or used to fashion rhubarb lemonade. The lemonade is a lovely pale pink. The rhubarb flavor is subtle but discernible, and the drink as a whole will refresh you on a hot day.

for the syrup:
3 cups rhubarb
2 cups sugar
2 cups water

for the lemonade:
3 tablespoons rhubarb syrup (see above)
3 tablespoons freshly squeezed lemon juice
water as needed

To make the syrup, combine the ingredients in a medium nonreactive saucepan. Bring the mixture to a boil; then reduce the heat and simmer for 25 minutes.

Strain the syrup through cheesecloth twice. You will end up with about 2-1/2 cups of syrup. Keep your syrup refrigerated.

To make a glass of lemonade, place 3 to 4 ice cubes in a 12-ounce glass. Add the 3 tablespoons of syrup, the lemon juice, and enough water to fill the glass. Stir. Serves 1.

Rhubarb Tea

This recipe for iced tea is in my Pudding Hollow Cookbook *so I didn't plan originally to include it here—but it is so popular when I do cooking demonstrations that I had to repeat it.*

The recipe originally came from my late neighbor Florette. Florette was glamorous and eccentric. She taught me a lot about rhubarb and a lot about life, and I'm grateful for those lessons.

for the rhubarb juice:
2 pounds rhubarb stalks, chopped (about 6 cups)
3 cups water
1 pinch salt

for the sugar syrup:
2 cups water
3/4 cup sugar

for assembly:
1 quart strong black tea

In a nonreactive saucepan, cook the rhubarb in the water, partially covered, over moderately low heat for 10 to 12 minutes or until tender. Stir gently on occasion to keep it from boiling. Cool slightly. Drain the rhubarb in a sieve placed over a bowl and set the pulp aside. Add the salt to the rhubarb juice.

In another saucepan, combine the ingredients for the sugar syrup. Bring the mixture to a boil, stirring and brushing the sugar crystals from the sides of the pan until the sugar is dissolved. Cook the syrup over moderate heat for 5 minutes; then remove it from the heat and let it cool.

To make rhubarb tea, combine 2 parts black tea, 1 part rhubarb juice, and 1 part sugar syrup. Serve in a tall glass over ice. As indicated, 4 cups tea, 2 cups rhubarb juice, and 2 cups sugar syrup make 2 quarts of tea.

Store any leftover juice or syrup in the refrigerator. If you need a double amount of sugar syrup, make 2 separate batches.

Wondering what to do with that rhubarb pulp? You may compost it—but it works wonders with copper pots! Soak your pot in it overnight, and it will look as though you spent hours polishing it in the morning. THEN compost the pulp.

Interlude: Advice from Florette on Picking Rhubarb

This isn't rocket science, but it's useful information, something I share with readers and television viewers every spring. The photo below depicts the glamorous Florette in her youth.

Take the following items to your rhubarb patch:

a knife
a bag (for the rhubarb stalks)
common sense

Pull the rhubarb stalks gently out of the ground at a horizontal angle. This enables them to come out of the root easily and encourages new rhubarb to grow. DO NOT cut the rhubarb.

After pulling out each stalk, use your knife to cut off the leaf (which is poisonous and therefore not something you want to bring into your kitchen). My neighbor David Rich cuts the leaves off with a machete-like motion that looks satisfying. I can't quite duplicate his cutting skill, but I do the best I can.

The leaves may be left in the patch to mulch the rhubarb plants (I find this easiest), or they may be placed in your compost. Remember, they are poisonous and shouldn't enter your home.

You may slice off the non-leaf end of the rhubarb stalk in the garden or in the house.

Take your rhubarb stalks into the kitchen, fill the sink with cool water, and soak the stalks for a couple of minutes to clean them. (Some stalks may require gentle scrubbing.) Let the stalks dry on paper towels (I suppose cloth towels would do as well; Florette didn't mention them so I stick with paper), trim off any rough or stringy bits, and then go to town cooking with your rhubarb.

Rhubarb Cordial

I have made cordials with raspberries, blueberries, blackberries, and sour cherries. So naturally I wondered whether a rhubarb cordial would work. It does!

You may add the cordial to a fruit salad, put it in goopy desserts like the trifle on page 84, or drink it as an after-dinner liqueur—what my mother used to call a "digestif." I can't guarantee that it will aid your digestion, but, given rhubarb's famed medicinal properties, it just might.

2 cups rhubarb
1 cup sugar
vodka as needed

Place the rhubarb in a 1-quart Mason jar. Pour the sugar in over it and stir well; then fill the jar with vodka, cover it, and place it in a cool, dark place. Gently shake and/or turn the bottle twice daily until the sugar dissolves. At the end of 6 weeks, strain out your cordial. This recipe makes 2 cups, more or less, depending on the juiciness of your rhubarb.

Rhubarb Salsa

Why wait for tomato season to make salsa when you have rhubarb? This recipe is simple and always makes a hit with my guests and classes. Like most salsas, it is best eaten the same day it is made. You may certainly hang on to it in the refrigerator for a day or two (no more!), but you'll have to drain it.

2 cups finely chopped rhubarb
1/2 inch ginger root, peeled and chopped
3 to 4 tablespoons minced sweet onion (e.g., red onion or Vidalia)
1 clove garlic, minced
1 yellow bell pepper, finely chopped
1 jalapeño pepper, seeded and chopped
1 handful cilantro, chopped
the juice of 1 lemon or 1 lime
2 teaspoons honey
salt to taste (about 1 teaspoon)

Place the rhubarb and the ginger in a medium nonreactive saucepan. Pour boiling water over them. Return the water just to a boil; then remove the pan from the heat. Drain the rhubarb and ginger, and pour cold water over them to stop them from cooking longer. Drain again.

In a bowl combine the rhubarb and ginger, the onion, the garlic, the peppers, and the cilantro.

In a small bowl combine the citrus juice and the honey. Stir in the salt. Add this liquid to the rhubarb mixture, and stir well.

Refrigerate the salsa for at least an hour before serving. Or just dig in! (Sometimes a person can't wait.)

Serve with chips; over crackers and cream cheese; or with chicken, pork, or fish. The salsa may also be combined with tortilla chips and cheddar cheese to make nachos.

Makes about 1-1/2 cups salsa.

Rhubarb and Bacon Compost

This spread is really a compote, but one of my dinner-party guinea pigs misheard me say that word, and I thought "compost" was a fun name.

The recipe is adapted from one I found on the Wisconsin Cheese website, maintained by the Wisconsin Milk Marketing Board. I have fond memories of spending a couple of early summers in Wisconsin with my family when my father was working on his doctoral dissertation at the University of Wisconsin at Madison. In June we feasted on three of my favorite foods—rhubarb, asparagus, and cheese.

I loved visiting the university's dairy bar and trying various flavors of ice cream. (I'm not sure whether this eatery still exists. I hope so.). I recall—whether this is an accurate recollection or not, I couldn't say—that milk flowed from the water fountains there. Small-child heaven!

The original compote recipe included spices, but I prefer just a few fresh herbs to let the flavors of the bacon, rhubarb, and onion shine. This compote is best eaten after it has chilled completely. It makes a delightful sweet-and-savory accompaniment to cheddar or Swiss cheese on crackers or toast. When I made it, I used local bacon from a smokehouse near my home, Pekarski's in South Deerfield, Massachusetts. The bacon flavor really dominates here so I urge you to use the best bacon you can find.

4 slices bacon
2 cups sweet onion slices
2 cups finely chopped rhubarb
3 tablespoons cider vinegar
3 tablespoons maple syrup
1/2 teaspoon fresh thyme
1 teaspoon (maybe a little more!) fresh chives

Fry the bacon in small pieces in a nonreactive skillet. Add the onion, and cook over low heat, stirring occasionally, for about 15 minutes, until the onion starts to caramelize. Stir frequently. Add the rhubarb, the vinegar, and the maple syrup. Continue to cook, stirring occasionally, until the rhubarb softens and most of the liquid evaporates.

The timing on this stage will vary depending on the toughness of your rhubarb. When I made the compote, breaking down the rhubarb took about 10 minutes.

Remove from heat and cool to room temperature. Stir in the herbs, and refrigerate until ready to use. Serve with cheese. This makes about 1-1/2 cups of compote.

A Hopeful Sign

Sides, Salads, and Breads

Rhubarb and Hope

Everyone has a favorite sign of spring. Yours may be a bird: a robin or a swallow. It may be a plant: a hyacinth or a pussy willow.

To me spring manifests itself in flavor: the flavor of rhubarb.

As a youngster I attended a Unitarian church with my family. We Unitarian children were vaguely aware of traditional religious holidays of spring like Easter and Passover. Nevertheless, to us Easter and Passover were times to celebrate the rebirth of the natural world rather than the resurrection of Christ or the flight of the Jews from Egypt.

I love a good Seder and a well composed Easter hymn, but I'm still a Unitarian at heart. I believe that spring is a time for celebrating nature's renaissance above all. This belief is bolstered by the fact that I live in a place that tends to get cold, snowy, and dark in the winter. My house is set between two ridges of hills so the short days are even shorter than they would otherwise be; the sun rises later and sets earlier than it would in a flat area.

I long to see the clumps of brown that gradually spread from the edges of the snow into the lawn until at long last winter's cloak of white is gone. I crave a vision of daffodils and apple blossoms popping out suddenly—their appearance always seems sudden—and bringing color to the landscape.

Most of all, I want to taste something fresh and very, very local. The first thing we get to taste from our yards in western Massachusetts is maple syrup. Taps and lines fill with sap, and local sugarhouses begin boiling, usually in February.

Next comes my favorite weed, the dandelion green (about which more later).

Finally, rhubarb stalks begin to push their way out of the ground, shouting "Spring!" with their vibrant color and tart flavor. It's a cliché to call rhubarb a harbinger of the season, but clichés often ring true. When I taste the year's first stewed rhubarb, I rejoice. Spring has arrived.

Rhubarb brings hope for all the foods and times to come as the sun gets higher in the sky: asparagus and strawberries and peaches, long walks through the woods with my dog, elongated afternoons of swimming and visiting, dinner parties that last into the lingering summer evenings.

Rhubarb may represent hope for the world as well as for the individuals who harvest and enjoy it. In the 1990s chemists at Yale discovered that oxalic acid, the substance that makes rhubarb stalks tart and rhubarb leaves poisonous, may help in the fight to rid the earth of built-up chlorofluorocarbons, those nasty chemicals that did damage to the ozone layer for decades.

I can't promise that rhubarb will save the world. I read about the chemists' discovery in a June 1996 article from *Discover* titled "Rhubarb to the Rescue." I haven't found a single article about the rhubarb-versus-chlorofluorocarbon battle that didn't cite the study from the 1990s. I therefore presume that no new research has been done.

Nevertheless, a girl can hope. I'll do my part for the world by continuing to grow and eat rhubarb as much as I can.

For Rhubarb Lovers Only

    I was a little hesitant to try this recipe. It involves … ahem! … grilling.
    I'm not generally a sexist, but there are certain things I'd just rather have men do. Change batteries on high smoke alarms (thank you, David!). Fasten the hose to the outdoor faucet so the water doesn't gush out (thank you, Will and Jack!).
    And grill.
    One evening a decade or so ago, however, the temperature was extremely warm, and no men were in sight. So I pulled out the grill and the charcoal and eventually got a fire going. My mother, the dog, and I enjoyed a marinated flank steak.
    Along with … grilled rhubarb!
    Ann Brauer, a quilt artist in Shelburne Falls, Massachusetts, knows of my passion for rhubarb. She told me that she enjoyed grilling it and suggested that I try this technique.
    I was skeptical. I have been known to lose pieces of chicken through the slots of the grill. I had a feeling I would end up with more rhubarb in the fire than on top of it.
    Ann told me that she had grilled her rhubarb on foil, however, which made the project much more doable.
    The grilling is a teensy bit tricky anyway. As I state in the recipe that follows, one wants the rhubarb to become slightly soft but not mushy. My first batch was a bit underdone; we could still see sugar adhering to the stalks. Finally, I managed to get just the right consistency.
    Warning: I know I've said that many of my rhubarb recipes will appeal to non-rhubarb fans. This is not one of those recipes. The tart rhubarb flavor comes through loud and clear.
    As rhubarb lovers, my mother and I were very, very happy. The dog even ate a couple of pieces. (My dogs have excellent taste.)
    I apologize for the vague proportions in the recipe that follows. My mother and I ate about 4 pieces of rhubarb each, but people with bigger appetites would probably eat many more.

Grilled Rhubarb

rhubarb to taste—washed, trimmed, and cut into 3-inch pieces

sugar as needed

Rinse the rhubarb pieces well and barely drain them. Leave a little water on your stalks so that the sugar will stick to them.

Pour sugar into a flat bowl, and roll the pieces of rhubarb in it.

Grill on foil over a not-too-hot grill, turning from time to time, until the sugar melts and the rhubarb starts to soften but doesn't completely lose its texture. On my grill this took about 15 minutes, but I am not a reliable griller. Keep an eye on your rhubarb and pay no attention to me!

Remove and serve.

Asparagus Risotto with Rhubarb

I adore risotto. It is delightfully rich and shows off just about any vegetable. It requires a fair amount of hands-on work in the kitchen; the rice relies on the gradual addition of stock (and constant stirring) to achieve maximum creaminess. I usually invite my dinner guests to relax with a drink in the kitchen while I prepare risotto; that way, I don't miss out on any of the pre-dinner conversation.

The rhubarb is an accent here—but a welcome one, giving both color and tang to the rice. Of the five rhubarb dishes I served to neighbors one evening when I was in a flurry of testing recipes, this won the popular vote hands down!

1 cup finely chopped rhubarb
2 teaspoons sugar
1/2 cup (1 stick) sweet butter
1 cup chopped onion
1-1/4 cups Arborio rice
3/4 cup white wine
1 cup uncooked asparagus pieces
1 cup chopped yellow bell pepper
4 cups simmering chicken stock, plus a little more (or a little water if you run out of stock) if needed
4 teaspoons chopped parsley
1/2 cup grated Parmesan cheese (plus a bit more if desired)
chopped fresh chives for garnish

Preheat the oven to 450 degrees. Place the rhubarb and the sugar in a bowl, toss them together, and let them sit for 10 minutes. Line a small rimmed baking sheet with foil, and roast the rhubarb on it for 5 minutes. Remove it from the oven and set it aside.

In a 4-quart Dutch oven, melt half of the butter and add the onion. Cook, stirring, for 5 minutes. Add the rice. Cook for 1 minute. Add 1/2 cup of the wine plus the asparagus and the bell pepper, and stir. Add 1 cup of stock. Keep stirring. As the mixture cooks and liquid is absorbed, add the remaining stock a bit at a time.

Cooking will take a while, somewhere between half an hour and 45 minutes. (In my experience, the only sure-fire way to know whether risotto is done is to taste it.) Just before serving, add the parsley, the remaining wine and butter, and the cheese. Place the risotto in a pretty bowl, and sprinkle the rhubarb pieces and the chives on top. Serves 6.

Strawberry-Rhubarb Spinach Salad

This is one of my favorite spring salads—full of contrasting flavors, textures, and colors. It looks as though it has a lot of steps, but the vinegar can be put together long in advance. The actual salad is quite manageable.

for the strawberry vinegar:
strawberries (don't use too many at a time or making the vinegar will take forever)
enough distilled white vinegar to cover them
equal amounts of sugar and water

for the salad:
1 cup chopped rhubarb
1 tablespoon sugar
1 tablespoon strawberry vinegar
salt and pepper to taste
2 tablespoons extra-virgin olive oil
4 cups spinach
toasted pecans to taste
feta cheese to taste

The Vinegar:

The day before you want to eat your salad (or any time up to a year earlier!), start the vinegar.

Place the berries in a nonreactive pan or dish. (A porcelain bowl works well.) Cover them with the vinegar, and leave them to soak, covered, overnight. If you forget them for a day and wait a couple of nights, they will still be fine.

The next day (or the day after that), gently strain the vinegary juice through cheesecloth. You may squeeze the berries a little, but don't overdo this; letting the juice drip out on its own is best.

Measure the juice. Then measure a little under 1-1/2 times as much sugar and water as juice (i.e., if you have a cup of juice, use just under 1-1/2 cups of sugar and 1-1/2 cups of water) into a saucepan.

Cook the sugar/water mixture until it threads. Measure the resultant sugar syrup. Add an equal quantity of the berry liquid to it, and boil the mixture for 10 minutes. Strain this boiled vinegar through cheesecloth, and decant it into sterilized bottles. Cork or cover. Stored in the dark, strawberry vinegar should keep its color and flavor for up to a year.

The Salad:

When you are ready to start your salad, preheat the oven to 450 degrees. While the oven is preheating toss the rhubarb and sugar together in a bowl, and let them sit for at least 10 minutes.

Line a rimmed baking sheet with foil, and place the sugared rhubarb pieces on it. Bake until the rhubarb just begins to soften, about 5 minutes. Remove the rhubarb from the oven and set it aside.

In a small bowl or jar combine the vinegar, the salt and pepper, and the oil.

Place the spinach in a salad bowl. Add the rhubarb, the pecans, and the feta; then remix the salad dressing and toss it into the salad. Serves 4 as a side salad.

Stump Sprouts Maple Rhubarb Cole Slaw

My neighbors Lloyd and Suzanne Crawford own Stump Sprouts. High on a hill in Hawley, Massachusetts, the Crawfords offer room and board to cross-country skiers, attendees of small conferences, family groups, and other visitors at their lodge.

Their guests are always fun. One afternoon last August, I found a message from Sue on my answering machine. She wanted to know whether I would be interested in coming to see a 40-minute version of Macbeth *at Stump Sprouts that afternoon.*

I couldn't figure out how anyone could make the Scottish Play that short ... so of course I went, and brought my neighbor Alice.

A group of drama students enthusiastically performed one scene from each of the play's five acts for us. Their passion for acting, and for the play's message about ambition and politics, proved hard to resist.

Lloyd and Suzanne are committed to sustainability. They have enough sunlight to generate their own solar electricity, and they serve home-grown (or local) foods to their guests as much as possible. Naturally, rhubarb is one of their favorites.

I asked Lloyd for a recipe. He came up with this clever, sweet-and-sour way to use two of my favorite local ingredients, maple syrup and rhubarb. Lloyd freezes batches of stewed rhubarb in the spring so that he can make this salad all year round.

1/2 cup extra-virgin olive oil
1/2 cup red-wine vinegar
1-1/2 tablespoons toasted sesame oil
1/3 cup stewed, unsweetened rhubarb (combine rhubarb with a small amount of water and a pinch of salt in a saucepan, and cook, stirring frequently, until it breaks down)
3 to 4 tablespoons maple syrup
salt and freshly cracked pepper to taste
1 medium green cabbage, finely shredded
toasted sunflower seeds to taste

In a jar, combine the olive oil, the vinegar, the sesame oil, the rhubarb, the maple syrup, and the salt and pepper. Cover and shake well. Toss this dressing together with the cabbage 20 minutes to 2 hours before serving. Garnish with the sunflower seeds.

This recipe may be cut in half or even into quarters. The coleslaw will be edible for a day or two before it gets too watery.

Serves 12 to 15.

Rhubarb Scones

This recipe stemmed from necessity. I went to my neighbor Dennis's garden one morning in early May determined to come back with rhubarb (with his permission, of course).

Unfortunately, the rhubarb was only just starting to emerge from the ground. I ended up with a tiny amount—about a cup and a half chopped.

I made scones with some of it and stewed the rest. I love stewed rhubarb. Well, I love rhubarb made just about any way.

These scones are buttery, with a nice balance of sweet and tart. And of course one could always add a little more rhubarb.

1 tablespoon plus 1/2 cup sugar
2/3 cup chopped rhubarb
2 cups flour
1-1/2 teaspoons baking power
1 teaspoon baking soda
1/2 teaspoon salt
1/2 cup (1 stick) cold sweet butter
1 egg
2/3 cup buttermilk
1 teaspoon vanilla
cinnamon sugar as needed

Preheat the oven to 350 degrees. Line 2 cookie sheets with parchment or silicone mats.

Sprinkle the tablespoon of sugar over the rhubarb. Stir. Let the mixture sit while you mix the dry ingredients.

Combine the 1/2 cup sugar, the flour, the baking powder, the baking soda, and the salt. Cut in the butter, but be careful not to over mix. Stir the rhubarb into this mixture. In a separate bowl, combine the egg, the buttermilk, and the vanilla. Add this liquid to the rhubarb mixture and blend just to moisten the dry ingredients.

Quickly scoop dough (it will be moist) into rounds on the prepared cookie sheets. Small rounds will give you about 16 small scones, but you may also make 8 larger scones. Sprinkle cinnamon sugar on top for added flavor and crunch.

Bake for 18 to 20 minutes for small scones or a bit longer for large ones. Makes 8 large or 16 small scones.

Sides, Salads, and Breads

Rhubarb Bread

This recipe is adapted from dairy producer Land o' Lakes. It makes a tasty morning loaf. It was one of the last gifts I took to my Uncle Bruce before he died in 2016 so it always makes me think of him—a smart, charming, ever curious man whom I miss.

for the bread:
1/2 cup (1 stick) sweet butter at room temperature
1 cup sugar
2 eggs
1/3 cup orange juice
1 tablespoon orange zest (optional but good)
1 teaspoon baking powder
1/4 teaspoon baking soda
1/4 teaspoon salt
2 cups flour
1-1/2 cups (generous) finely chopped rhubarb

for the streusel:
1/4 cup flour
1/4 cup brown sugar, firmly packed
2 teaspoons cinnamon
2 tablespoons sweet butter

Preheat the oven to 350 degrees. Grease and flour a standard loaf pan, or spray it with a spray that both greases and flours. (You may also grease and flour 3 small loaf pans, which make lovely gifts for individuals.)

In a mixing bowl cream together the butter and the sugar. Beat in the eggs, 1 at a time, followed by the orange juice and the zest if you are using it. (Don't worry if the mixture looks a bit curdled.) Beat in the baking powder, the baking soda, and the salt. On low speed, stir in the flour; then fold in the rhubarb by hand.

In a bowl combine the flour, the brown sugar, and the cinnamon for the streusel; then cut in the butter or rub it in with your fingers.

Spoon half of the bread batter into the prepared loaf pan or pans. Top with half of the streusel. Spoon in the remaining bread batter, followed by the remaining streusel.

Bake the bread until a toothpick inserted into the center comes out clean, about 55 to 70 minutes for the large loaf or 30 to 40 minutes for the small loaves. (The baking time will depend on your pan and your oven.)

Cool the bread in its pan(s) for 10 minutes; then gently loosen the sides and remove the bread. Let it cool on a rack. Once the bread has cooled, wrap it in foil until ready to serve. Makes 1 large loaf or 3 small ones.

Sides, Salads, and Breads

Rhubarb Sugar-Top Muffins

Who doesn't love a sweet muffin in the morning? This recipe is adapted from a blueberry formula supplied to me by a musical acquaintance named Theresa Kubasak, who obtained it from a teaching nun named Gen Cassani. My nephew Michael wolfed down several of these muffins the morning I first made them.

One could argue that as a teenager he will wolf down pretty much anything, of course, but his parents managed to eat them pretty quickly as well.

2 cups chopped rhubarb (fairly small pieces work best)
2 tablespoons confectioner's sugar
1/2 cup (1 stick) sweet butter
2 cups flour
1 cup sugar
2 teaspoons baking powder
1/2 teaspoon salt
1/2 cup milk
2 eggs
sanding sugar (or regular sugar if that's all you have) as needed

Preheat the oven to 350 degrees. Toss the rhubarb in the confectioner's sugar and set it aside. Melt the butter, and set it aside as well.

In a medium bowl combine the dry ingredients. Stir in the milk and then the eggs, one at a time. Stir in the melted butter, followed by the sugared rhubarb. Use a cookie scoop or a tablespoon to spoon the batter into lined muffin tins. Sprinkle sugar generously on top.

Bake until the muffins begin to brown on top and pass the toothpick test, 20 to 25 minutes. Makes 18 to 24 small muffins.

Susan Purdy's Healthy and Delicious Rhubarb Muffins

If the previous recipe relied a little too heavily on white flour and sugar for your taste, these muffins are for you. Personally, I love both recipes. These muffins are great for breakfast but also terrific to serve with dinner. My neighbor Susan Purdy supplied the recipe. She notes that the rhubarb puree is delicious served on the side of pork tenderloin.

for the rhubarb puree:
4 cups rhubarb
4 teaspoons freshly chopped ginger
1/4 cup honey
1 tablespoon water

for the muffins:
3/4 cup wheat bran
1 cup whole-wheat flour
1/3 cup sugar
2 teaspoons cinnamon
1 teaspoon baking powder
1 teaspoon baking soda
1/2 cup raisins
1 cup rhubarb puree
1 egg, lightly beaten
1/2 cup buttermilk
1/4 cup vegetable oil

First, make your rhubarb puree. Place the puree ingredients in a microwave-safe bowl that is quite a bit larger than the ingredients. Cover the bowl loosely with plastic wrap, and microwave on high for 4 minutes. Remove the plastic wrap, stir, and cook for 2 to 3 minutes more. (Watch for overflowing!) This recipe makes about 2 cups of puree so you should be able to make more than 1 batch of muffins.

When you are ready to start the muffins, preheat the oven to 400 degrees. Grease 12 to 18 muffin tins or line them with cupcake liners. (Susan usually makes 12 muffins; I ended up with 18.)

In a bowl, combine the dry ingredients. Stir in the raisins. Whisk together the wet ingredients in another bowl. Pour the wet ingredients into the dry, and stir until the mixture is barely combined.

Bake the muffins until a toothpick inserted into the middle comes out clean, about 20 to 25 minutes. Makes 12 to 18 small muffins.

Main Dishes and Condiments

Forcing Rhubarb

One tradition that no longer holds much sway in the United States is the custom of "forcing" rhubarb in winter. A few farms in the Pacific Northwest, such as the Richter Family Farm in Puyallup, Washington, still engage in this practice.

Forced rhubarb is best known in Britain, primarily in a Yorkshire area known as the Rhubarb Triangle. This nine-square-mile stretch lies between the towns of Leeds, Wakefield, and Bradford.

E. Oldroyd & Sons, prominent Yorkshire rhubarb producers, say on their website that rhubarb first became a popular winter crop in Yorkshire in 1877.

Forced rhubarb is cultivated outdoors for two years and then moved in the fall into indoor forcing sheds. The sheds are heated to tropical temperatures.

The rhubarb grows in darkness in the warm sheds until January or February. The heat makes the rhubarb grow extra fast. Growers claim that they can actually hear the rhubarb pop as it grows. I don't believe everything I find on the internet, but YouTube does in fact feature several audio clips of popping rhubarb in forcing sheds.

At winter's height, the rhubarb is harvested by candlelight. The darkness in the sheds keeps the rhubarb a bright red. (Think of the green rhubarb one finds in home patches in the fall, thanks to photosynthesis from the summer sun.) The darkness and heat supposedly give the rhubarb extra delicacy and sweetness as well. I haven't ever tasted forced rhubarb so I am obliged to take the word of the Yorkshire growers on this.

In the mid-20th century a special train known as the Rhubarb Express left the Rhubarb Triangle nightly to deliver stalks of rhubarb to market gardens in London. Not a lot of fresh fruit was available in February then so the rhubarb was highly prized.

The rhubarb sheds are disappearing from the Yorkshire landscape just as my native Pioneer Valley is losing its historic tobacco barns. Nevertheless, the dwindling tradition of the candlelight rhubarb harvest is still treasured by the remaining growers and by rhubarb lovers in the area and beyond. In fact, the rhubarb sheds are now a tourist attraction.

The growers hold an annual Festival of Food, Drink, and Rhubarb each February to celebrate their heritage and attract new rhubarb fans. The Oldroyds offer tours of their forcing sheds to the public between January and March. One family member, Janet Oldroyd Hulme, is known as the High Priestess of Rhubarb. Hulme has won awards for, in the words of her local regional food group, "almost single-handedly raising the profile of Yorkshire rhubarb from that of humble school dinner status to that of super food, and celebrity chef favorite."

Several years ago Hulme and others lobbied for, and were granted, "protected designation of origin" status for Yorkshire rhubarb from the European Union. This means that rhubarb must be from Yorkshire in order to be called Yorkshire rhubarb. The Yorkshire rhubarb is in good company: other protected foods include Champagne, Gorgonzola cheese, and Prosciutto.

Someday I hope to journey to Yorkshire to experience the Festival of Food, Drink, and Rhubarb in person. Meanwhile, Simon Simpson of the Wakefield Council, which organizes this annual event, sent me a chicken recipe from Chef Rachel Green, which was served at a recent festival.

It appears here as I adapted it, along with a few other recipes for main dishes and condiments. Rhubarb isn't just for dessert, after all.

As you prepare and eat them, I hope you'll ponder the idea of forcing rhubarb. I think it presents lessons to us all: to attempt the unexpected and reap sweet rewards. And to celebrate life's force even in the middle of winter.

Persian Rhubarb Stew with Chicken

Here is the rhubarb recipe sent to me by Simon Simpson, who works on events in Wakefield, Yorkshire. The combination of spices and flavors is unusual and appealing.

olive oil as needed for sautéing
1 large onion, sliced
4 garlic cloves, peeled and crushed
1 teaspoon turmeric
2 teaspoons cinnamon
6 chicken thighs
1 cup rich chicken stock
1 large bunch chopped flat-leaf parsley
1 bunch chopped mint leaves
1/2 teaspoon saffron threads, crushed into powder and mixed with 2 tablespoons hot water
1 cup raisins (optional but good)
salt and pepper to taste
3 cups rhubarb, cut into 1-inch pieces

Heat 2 tablespoons of oil in a 4-quart Dutch oven over medium heat. Add the onion slices and sauté until they are soft. Add the garlic, the turmeric, the cinnamon, and the chicken pieces. Stir to coat the chicken in the spices. Add the stock, and bring the mixture to a boil. Once the stock is boiling, turn the heat to low and cook for 10 minutes, uncovered.

Meanwhile, heat 2 to 3 tablespoons of olive oil in a frying pan over medium-high heat. Add the parsley and the mint, and cook, stirring continuously, until the parsley is soft (3 to 5 minutes). Be careful not to burn the parsley. Add the herbs to the chicken, along with the saffron water and the raisins if you are using them. Season with salt and pepper, and stir to mix. Scatter the rhubarb on top.

Continue to cook until the chicken is done and the rhubarb is tender, about 30 minutes.

Taste and adjust seasonings as needed. Serve with plain basmati rice, Greek yogurt, and a few more mint leaves. Serves 4 to 6.

First-Prize Rhubarb Chili

Linda Stephenson and her husband Sonny have run L & S Gardens in La Pine, Oregon, for almost three decades. For several years, Linda has organized La Pine's annual rhubarb festival, a day of contests, sales, and rhubarb. Linda comes from generations of farmers and adores rhubarb; it was she who gave me the idea of making rhubarb salsa.

In 2016 La Pine's Rhubarb Festival included a chili contest. I asked Linda for the winning recipe, which she kindly supplied. I was a little suspicious when I noticed that the contest was won by the person who was then La Pine's mayor, Ken Mulenex. When my family tasted the chili, however, we decided that Mr. Mulenex had won fair and square. It's hard to taste the rhubarb in this dish—which is a plus for some people and a minus for others.

The mayor cooked his chili outdoors over charcoal, but I made it on my stove top, which worked just fine. One may vary the spices to taste; this is a hearty, not-too-hot chili.

1-1/2 pounds lean ground beef
1 large onion, chopped
1 medium green bell pepper, chopped
1 jalapeño pepper, chopped
2 cloves garlic, minced
3 cups rhubarb, chopped
1 large (28- or 29-ounce) can crushed tomatoes
1 tablespoon chili powder (or to taste)
1/8 teaspoon cayenne pepper (or to taste)
1 bay leaf
2 (15-ounce) cans pinto beans
salt and pepper to taste
masa harina for thickening (Mayor Mulenex uses Bob's Red Mill brand)

In a large heavy pot brown the beef. Remove it from the pot and place it in a bowl lined with paper towels to drain off some of the fat. Keep about 3 tablespoons of fat in the pot and sauté the onion, the peppers, the garlic, and the rhubarb for about 5 minutes, until the onion pieces are translucent.

Add the tomatoes and the spices. Stir to combine, and bring the mixture to a boil. Reduce heat to medium (325 degrees if you are using a grill), and cook for 1 hour, adding a little water if the chili gets too dry. (The mayor didn't specify whether to cover the pot so I covered it in part.)

Add the pinto beans, undrained, during the last 5 to 7 minutes of cooking. Stir in a little masa harina to give the chili body.

The mayor says that this chili serves 4 to 6—but in my family (we served it with rice) it served 6 to 8.

> **2 FLUID OZS.**
> **DR. THACHER'S**
> **LAXATIVE COMPOUND OF**
> **SENNA AND RHUBARB**
> Active Ingredients: Senna and Indian Rhubarb, not U.S.P.
> Inactive Ingredients: Spigelia, glycerin, aromatics, corn syrup, sodium benzoate U.S.P., acid salicylic U.S.P., caramel and water.
> **THACHER MEDICINE COMPANY**
> 16th & Gulf Streets   Chattanooga, Tenn.

Rhubarb–Glazed Meatballs

As you'll see elsewhere in this book, I sometimes adapt cranberry recipes for rhubarb use. Cranberries and rhubarb are similar in flavor, and it seems hard to wait for fall to use all my cranberry recipes!

Cranberry-glazed meatballs appear in community cookbooks everywhere; they are easy to make, and the sweetness of the sauce makes them popular. The meatballs can serve either as an appetizer or as a main course.

1 pound lean ground beef
1/3 cup finely chopped onion
1 garlic clove, finely minced
1/3 cup dried bread crumbs
1/2 teaspoon salt
1/8 teaspoon black pepper
2 eggs, slightly beaten
1 12-ounce bottle chili sauce
2-3/4 cups stewed rhubarb, pureed in a blender (see page 83 for basic recipe)

Preheat the oven to 375 degrees. In a large bowl combine all the ingredients except the chili sauce and the rhubarb.

Mix well; then shape the mixture into 1-inch balls. Place the balls on a large rimmed baking sheet, and bake for 25 to 30 minutes (or until done). While the meatballs are baking, combine the chili sauce and the rhubarb in a 3-quart nonreactive saucepan. Bring them to a simmer and cook for 5 minutes, stirring frequently.

When the meatballs are done add them to the sauce. Stir to coat, and simmer for 5 more minutes, stirring gently from time to time.

Makes about 24 meatballs.

Rhubarb Pizza

I admit it: my family thought I was a little crazy to try to make pizza with rhubarb. My first attempt didn't reassure them; it was simultaneously too sweet and too tart and had an odd consistency. This final version made just about everyone who tried it happy, however. It may be served as a main course or cut into small pieces as an appetizer. It's light—as you can see, it doesn't use a lot of any one ingredient—and very attractive.

for the sauce:
a splash of extra-virgin olive oil
1/2 large red onion, thinly sliced
2 garlic scapes, chopped, or 1 large garlic clove, minced
1 cup chopped rhubarb
1-1/2 teaspoons honey
1/2 teaspoon salt
a few turns of the pepper grinder

for the rest of the pizza:
1 medium pizza crust (I used a 20-ounce crust)
extra-virgin olive oil as needed
4 ounces feta cheese, crumbled
1/2 pound fresh spinach (a little more if you like)
1 garlic scape, chopped, or 1 garlic clove, minced

A couple of days before you plan to make the pizza, heat the oil for the sauce in a Dutch oven or frying pan. Toss in the onion slices and pieces of garlic, and cook them over low heat until they begin to caramelize (probably 20 minutes to 1/2 hour), adding a very small amount of water if necessary to keep the vegetables from sticking to the pan.

Toss in the rhubarb, the honey, the salt, and the pepper, and continue to cook over medium-low heat until the rhubarb is tender but not completely broken down, about 8 to 10 minutes.

Let the sauce cool to room temperature, put it in a covered container, and let it sit in the refrigerator for 2 days. When you open the container you will find that the onions have taken on a lovely bright pink color from the rhubarb.

A couple of hours before you are ready to make the pizza, take your crust out of the refrigerator (if you are using a commercial crust; if your crust is homemade, it will be at room temperature). Place it on a greased baking sheet, and let it rest. After an hour and a half or so, preheat the oven to 475 degrees, and stretch the crust out on the baking sheet.

Lightly oil the top of the crust, and spread the rhubarb sauce on top. It doesn't have to cover the crust; this is a simple savory pizza, not a heavy one.

Sprinkle the cheese on top, and bake the pizza until it looks done, 10 to 12 minutes.

While the pizza is baking, sauté the spinach and the garlic in olive oil over medium heat until the spinach wilts. Set this mixture aside.

When the pizza comes out of the oven, sprinkle the spinach mixture on top. Let the pizza rest for a minute or two; then slice it. Serves 4 as a main course or more as a snack or appetizer.

Main Dishes and Condiments

Persian Lamb and Rhubarb Stew

This recipe comes from Kristin Nicholas of Leyden Glen Farm in Leyden, Massachusetts. She and her husband Mark Duprey have been raising sheep since 1980, and she loves to experiment with lamb recipes. Kristin also makes this recipe with bone-in lamb meat (removing the bones when she shreds the meat).

When I made the stew, my guests raved. The blend of spices is intriguing, yet the lamb flavor comes through loud and clear. I would make it again in a heartbeat.

1 large onion, chopped
4 cloves garlic, minced
3 tablespoons olive oil
1-1/2 teaspoons coriander seeds, cracked
1 teaspoon cumin seeds
1/2 teaspoon cinnamon
1 teaspoon ground ginger
1/2 teaspoon nutmeg
1 pound lamb stew meat
1 small can (14 ounces) Italian tomatoes
salt and freshly ground pepper to taste
water or lamb stock as needed
1 pound rhubarb, cut into 1-inch pieces (about 3 cups)
1/2 cup golden raisins
2 tablespoons honey
1/4 cup minced fresh mint or parsley or a mixture of the two

In a 4-quart Dutch oven, brown the onion and the garlic in 2 tablespoons of the olive oil until the onion pieces are translucent. Add the coriander, the cumin, the cinnamon, the ginger, and the nutmeg. Cook until the spices begin to smell lovely. If the mixture begins to stick, add a tiny bit of water to create a little sauce. Remove the onion mixture from the pan and set it aside.

Add the remaining tablespoon of olive oil to the pan. Brown the lamb on all sides. Remove the lamb from the pan and set it aside; then discard the excess fat from the pan. Return the onion mixture and the lamb to the Dutch oven.

Add the tomatoes, the salt, and the pepper. Add water (or lamb stock) to the pot so that it covers the lamb halfway.

Bring the stew to a boil on top of the stove. Cover the pot with a tight-fitting lid, place it in a 250-degree oven and cook for 3 hours.

At the end of the three hours, remove the meat from the pot and try to shred some with the tines of a fork. If the meat is not tender and shred-able, return it to the oven. Check it periodically until it is tender.

With your hands, shred the meat; it should be falling apart into chunks. Add the sliced rhubarb, the chunks of cooked meat, the raisins, and the honey to the pot. Bring the pot to a boil on the top of the stove; then return it to the oven to cook, covered, for another hour.

Remove the stew from the oven and taste it. Add more spices if you want a more intense flavor. If the flavor is too sour, add a touch more honey. If the stew is too saucy, simmer it with the lid off to reduce the liquid.

The flavor of this stew improves if it sits in the fridge for a couple of days. Serve over basmati rice, couscous, or rice pilaf garnished with the parsley and/or mint. Serves 4 to 6.

Swordfish Steak with Rhubarb Salsa

Actually, you may pair rhubarb salsa with just about any fish (it's also great with chicken cutlets), but I like this particular combination. My friend Kate Pyle Bryda taught me the mayonnaise technique; it keeps the swordfish beautifully moist.

4 swordfish steaks, about 1-inch thick
mayonnaise as needed (up to 1/2 cup)
salt, pepper, and lemon juice to taste
lots of rhubarb salsa (see page 24) for garnish

Heat up your grill—or get out a grill pan. (I prefer the outdoor method, but sometimes it rains!)

Coat the swordfish steaks with mayonnaise on both sides, and sprinkle them with salt, pepper, and lemon juice.

Place the steaks on the grill and cook until the fish loses its translucency but is still moist, about 10 minutes, turning once.

Serve the fish with mounds of salsa. Makes 4 servings.

Aunt Lura

Aunt Lura's Rhubarb Chutney

This delightful side spread is more a conserve than a chutney; it is sweet and fruity rather than spicy. It's based on a cranberry recipe my aunt makes every year. I enjoy it on the side of broiled chicken or pork—or as a spread with crackers and cream cheese.

1/4 cup orange juice
4 cups chopped rhubarb
1 peeled, seeded orange, cut into chunks
2 cups sugar
1 cup chopped peeled and cored apple
1/2 cup raisins
1/2 cup walnuts, chopped (optional)
1 tablespoon cider vinegar
1/2 teaspoon ground ginger
1/2 teaspoon cinnamon

Place all the ingredients in a nonreactive saucepan and cook until tender. Ladle the chutney into sterilized jars and process in a boiling-water bath for 10 minutes. Or just keep the mixture refrigerated. Makes 4 to 5 cups.

Toni's Spicy Rhubarb Chutney

Two rhubarb chutneys might seem like overkill, but this recipe is a different kettle of jam from its predecessor. It's much hotter, much more of a traditional chutney. I served it with curry to great acclaim.

The recipe comes from my former school classmate at the Beard School in New Jersey, Toni Sisto Klohr. Toni sometimes adds black pepper to the recipe. I haven't tried that—but I'd be willing to next time!

1-1/2 cups chopped rhubarb
1/2 cup packed light brown sugar
6 tablespoons finely chopped onion
1/4 cup cider vinegar
1/4 cup raisins or currants
1/2 teaspoon curry powder (1/4 teaspoon if using very hot curry powder)
1 pinch cinnamon (optional)
1 teaspoon finely chopped ginger root
1 clove garlic, chopped
1/4 teaspoon salt
1 pat of butter

Combine the ingredients in a medium nonreactive saucepan. Bring the mixture to a boil, turn it down, and simmer it until it thickens and comes together, stirring occasionally.

Ladle the chutney into sterilized jars. Cover and seal the jars, and then turn them upside down to cool completely. Or just refrigerate the chutney until you are ready to eat it.

Makes 1 pint (2 cups). This recipe may be doubled. If you're wondering why the cinnamon is optional, the explanation is simple. I put it in by accident; Toni doesn't use it. I liked it.

Tangy Rhubarb Barbecue Sauce

This sauce is everything barbecue sauce should be: flavorful, a little sweet, a little spicy. And it's made with rhubarb! It was created by Canadian home economist Getty Stewart (of www.gettystewart.com), who kindly gave me permission to use it.

a splash of canola oil
1/2 cup diced onion (about half a medium onion)
2 cloves garlic, minced
2 cups rhubarb, diced
1/4 cup water
1/2 cup brown sugar
1/2 cup tomato sauce
1/4 cup cider vinegar
2 tablespoons Dijon mustard
1 tablespoon chili powder
1/2 teaspoon cayenne pepper
1 tablespoon Worcestershire sauce
1/2 teaspoon salt (plus a little more if you can't resist)
1/4 teaspoon black pepper

In a large nonreactive saucepan heat the oil over medium heat. Add the onion and the garlic, and sauté until they are glassy but not brown (4 to 5 minutes). Add the rhubarb and the water. Cook, stirring from time to time, for 5 minutes or until the rhubarb starts to soften.

Add all of the remaining ingredients except the salt and the pepper. Bring the mixture to a boil; then reduce the heat and simmer the sauce for 20 to 30 minutes. The sauce should reduce quite a bit, and the flavors should meld.

Remove the sauce from the heat, and puree it with an immersion blender. (I like to leave it just a little lumpy rather than render it completely smooth.) If you don't have an immersion blender, use a regular one—but puree in batches. Add the salt and the pepper, and adjust the seasonings to taste; add cayenne for more heat, sugar for more sweetness, vinegar for more tang.

Store in the refrigerator for 7 to 10 days or freeze for up to 6 months. Makes about 2 cups.

Rhubarb Catch Up

I'm not exactly a champion griller. In fact, as listeners to New England Public Radio, a local radio station, learned a few years ago, I've been known to light an outdoor fire that almost turned into … well … an outdoor fire. Only my dog's fierce barking led me to peek outside at my preheating grill and rush to douse the flames.

Condiments for grilled foods I can manage, however. And so perhaps it was inevitable that I would make rhubarb ketchup (or catsup or catch up or however you spell it). I've tried a couple of different formulas, and this is the best. It doesn't taste like tomato ketchup. Why should it? It's a lightly sweet/lightly spiced sauce, nice with pork, chicken, or a hamburger.

3 cups finely chopped rhubarb
1/2 cup brown sugar, firmly packed
1/4 cup apple cider plus 1/2 cup later
3 tablespoons cider vinegar
1/4 teaspoon (generous) ground ginger
1/4 teaspoon cinnamon
1 pinch allspice
1/2 teaspoon pickling spices
1/2 teaspoon salt
a few turns of the pepper grinder

In a 2-quart nonreactive saucepan, toss together the rhubarb and the brown sugar. In a tiny saucepan, heat the 1/4 cup of cider and the vinegar. When they come to a boil remove them from the heat and stir in the spices.

Let the two pans sit at room temperature for 2 hours. The rhubarb should juice up a little, and the spices should steep.

After steeping, add the spices and their liquid to the rhubarb. Toss the remaining cider into the pot that held the spices to pick up any remaining bits, and add it to the rhubarb, too. Stir in the salt and the pepper. Bring the rhubarb mixture to a boil. Reduce the heat and boil, stirring frequently, for 20 minutes. Turn off the stove, and let the rhubarb cool.

In a blender or food processor, puree the cooled ketchup. Ladle it into a sterilized jar or two and refrigerate it until you are ready to use it. I don't know for sure how long this sauce will last in the refrigerator since my family ate it fairly quickly. I would recommend trying to use it up within a couple of weeks just to be sure. Makes about 2-1/2 cups of catch up.

Paula's Raspberry Rhubarb Jam

My neighbor Leslie Clark is generous with rhubarb; she has shared both fresh and frozen stalks with me for recipe testing. Sadly (because Leslie has a huge rhubarb patch), she doesn't do a lot with rhubarb herself. This jam is an exception to that rule. She likes to make several batches a year and reports that her houseguests and friends request it regularly. The jam tastes more like raspberries than like rhubarb, but that doesn't seem to bother Leslie's gift recipients.

The recipe originally comes from Paula Rice, the longtime mainstay of the meat department at Avery's Store, our local general emporium. Paula has been working at Avery's on and off since I was a teenager. She knows everyone who shops there and has a wicked sense of humor. She also knows her way around a kitchen.

5 cups chopped rhubarb
5 cups sugar
1 20-ounce can crushed pineapple, drained
1 pint raspberries
3 3-ounce boxes raspberry gelatin

Combine the rhubarb, the sugar, the pineapple, and the raspberries in a large nonreactive pot. Bring the mixture to a boil. Reduce the heat, and simmer for 45 minutes.

Stir in the gelatin. Cook until the jam just begins to boil again. Ladle the jam into sterilized jars, and seal. There is no need to process the jam, says Paula. Makes 8 to 9 cups.

Tinky's Rhubarb Jam

This jam formula is much more rhubarby—but less red! —than Paula's version.

4 cups chopped rhubarb
3 cups sugar (slightly less if you like)
the juice of 1/2 lemon
1 small pat butter

In a nonreactive pot combine the rhubarb, 2 cups of the sugar, and the lemon juice. Let them sit for an hour or so to juice up.

Over medium heat, cook the mixture, stirring frequently, until the rhubarb begins to soften; then stir in the remaining sugar and the butter. Cook, continuing to stir frequently, until the jam registers about 218 degrees on a candy thermometer or sheets off a cool stainless-steel spoon.

Remove the jam from the heat, and stir it for 5 minutes to distribute the rhubarb. Ladle it into sterilized 1/2-pint jars, seal, and process in a boiling-water bath for 5 minutes. Makes 2-1/2 to 3 cups of jam.

Rhubarb Curd

I thought I was original in coming up with the idea for rhubarb curd—and then I looked at the internet (always a humbling experience!). Variations on this recipe abound there ... for good reason.

This version is less attractive than lemon or lime curd; the rhubarb can end up sort of brownish, and the consistency isn't entirely smooth. The flavor makes up for any faults you may find in the appearance. The rhubarb and key-lime juice provide a deep, smooth tartness, and the eggs and butter make the whole thing rich and creamy. This curd is great with biscuits or scones. It may also be used instead of jam in jelly-roll cake. (See page 108.)

1 cup sugar, divided
2 cups chopped rhubarb
2 tablespoons key-lime juice
2 eggs
1 pinch salt
1/4 cup (1/2 stick) sweet butter, cut into chunks

In a nonreactive saucepan sprinkle 1/4 cup of the sugar over the chopped rhubarb. Let it sit at room temperature, covered, for several hours.

Bring the rhubarb mixture to a boil over medium heat. Cook until the rhubarb softens completely, adding a little water if necessary to keep the rhubarb from sticking to the bottom of the pan. Remove the rhubarb from the heat, and let it cool for a few minutes. Add the key-lime juice, and puree the mixture with a spoon, an immersion blender, or a whisk. It won't be completely smooth, but it will taste divine.

In a bowl whisk together the eggs and the remaining sugar. Add this mixture to the cooled rhubarb; then cook the combination, stirring, until it thickens and coats a spoon (about 8 minutes). Just before turning off the heat, stir in the salt.

Remove the curd from the heat and stir in the butter, a piece at a time, until it is incorporated.

Ladle into jars and refrigerate. Makes about 2 cups.

Rhubarb Chipotle Sauce

I first encountered chipotle sauce with raspberries. Since then I have made strawberry chipotle sauce, cranberry chipotle sauce, and peach chipotle sauce. Could rhubarb chipotle sauce be far behind? The combination of sweet and spicy in this recipe really pops. The sauce works well with pork or chicken—or over crackers with cream cheese. You could add other ingredients—onions, garlic—but why bother? The sauce works with two basic flavors, rhubarb and chipotle.

2 cups chopped rhubarb
1-1/2 cups sugar
the juice of 1/2 lemon
1 pinch salt
1 chipotle from a can of chipotles in adobo sauce (plus a little of the sauce), chopped, plus a little more chipotle and/or sauce if you love spice
1 pat butter

In a nonreactive pot combine the rhubarb, 1 cup of the sugar, and the lemon juice. Let the mixture sit for an hour or so to allow the rhubarb to juice up.

Add the remaining sugar, the salt, the chipotle, and the butter. Cook the mixture over low heat until tender, stirring frequently.

When the rhubarb has broken down, remove the sauce from the heat. Let it cool for a few minutes. Puree the sauce with a regular or immersion blender, but don't overdo this; a few lumps won't hurt.

Refrigerate the sauce after it cools. Makes about 1-1/2 cups.

"The Rhubarb Girl."

My late mother shared my love of asparagus.

A Green Digression

Dandelion Greens and Asparagus

Much as I love rhubarb, even I have to admit that man (and woman) cannot live by rhubarb alone. Even at the height of rhubarb season, I feel the need to supplement it. Happily, two of my favorite green vegetables come into season just before and just after rhubarb shows up in the yard.

The first is the humble dandelion green. Many years ago, I interviewed a practical farm wife named Rachel Kelley about her cooking practices. I asked Rachel to identify the very first thing she ate out of the ground every spring. She didn't have to think about the question. "Dandelion greens," she shot back.

I didn't actually try the greens myself, however, until several years later. David Rich, the neighbor who was cutting my lawn at the time, finished the first mowing of the year and appeared at my door in the spring of 2015. "I left you the dandelions by your herbs," he said. I must have looked perplexed because he clearly felt the need to elaborate. "I thought you might want to eat them," he added.

I don't hate dandelions as some people do. I certainly wouldn't poison the grass to get rid of them. Despite Rachel's story, it had never occurred to me to eat them. Still, I'm always ready to try something new. And goodness knows I had plenty of dandelions with which to experiment. My yard is awash with them every spring.

From then on I was a dandelion-green convert.

"Convert" is too mild a word to apply to my feelings about asparagus.

When I'm asked one of those hypothetical food questions—"What foods would you take with you to a desert island?" or "What would you choose to eat for your last meal on death row?"—I have no trouble making a decision. After rhubarb, I hone in on asparagus.

Of course, asparagus is a cool-climate plant and therefore unlikely to grow on a desert island. And a prison chef would probably cook it until it was soggy. Nevertheless, I could eat even soggy asparagus every day and be reasonably happy.

In May and June this vegetable is everywhere here in the Pioneer Valley. As David Nussbaum recalled a few years ago in an article in *Saveur*, the Connecticut River Valley was the world's asparagus capital between the 1930s and the 1970s.

Hadley Grass, as it was called, was shipped throughout the northeast and occasionally even overseas. It was purportedly enjoyed by the Royal Family at Buckingham Palace.

When a blight infected the crop in the mid-1970s, Nussbaum wrote, asparagus in the area was hard hit. It took a while to find a blight-resistant strain, and many farmers moved on. Today it is mostly locals who enjoy what remains of this formerly dominant crop.

Many western Massachusetts asparagus fans still use the term Hadley Grass, adapted from Sparrow Grass, a popular nickname for the vegetable in the 1700s and 1800s. Lexicographer John Walker wrote in the 1790s, "Sparrow grass is so general that *asparagus* has an air of stiffness and pedantry." (Emphasis mine.)

I was six or seven when I first realized how much I loved fresh asparagus. My family was visiting one of my father's graduate-school professors in Wisconsin. Like many midwesterners, Carl Bagholt and his wife Julia cultivated a huge garden.

When I took my first bite of the Bagholts' freshly harvested asparagus, I was amazed at its flavor and texture. It tasted more like butter than any vegetable should. I kept eating … and eating … and eating. Professor Bagholt eyed me with academic interest as he filled my plate. He had probably never seen a little girl who could eat such quantities of asparagus. I have a feeling he was wondering at what point I would turn green and explode.

I haven't consumed that much asparagus at one sitting since, but I still remember that visit with pleasure. And I celebrate asparagus season every year.

Here I offer a couple of recipes for each of rhubarb's companions to help readers supplement the red stalks with a little green.

Sautéed Dandelion Greens

David Rich, he of the lawn mower, told me that he and his wife Sally like to cook dandelion greens as they do spinach. My favorite way of cooking spinach (aside from making it into a salad) is to sauté it with a little olive oil and garlic so I opted for that method.

When I looked up edible dandelion greens on the internet, I saw a recipe for dandelion-green salad with walnut oil. Since I had some walnut oil in the house (I love it in salad dressing), I decided to spritz a bit onto my cooked greens. I didn't use it to cook them; walnut oil has a low smoking point.

1 large bunch dandelion greens (cut when they are young and tender, before the flowers come out)
a small amount of olive oil (start with 1 to 2 teaspoons and add a little more if needed)
1 clove garlic, cut into very thin strips
salt to taste
2 shakes of walnut oil
a few toasted walnuts (optional)

Soak the greens in cold water for a few minutes. While they are soaking remove any grass stalks that adhere to them. Place them in a colander to drain, but do not shake them dry; they should still be slightly damp when you cook them.

In a 12-inch sauté pan warm the olive oil over medium-high heat. Sauté the garlic pieces until they begin to turn golden brown.

Toss in the greens. They will sizzle a little because they are damp. Sauté them with the garlic just until they wilt. This is a rapid process.

Toss on salt to taste. Transfer the vegetables to a medium bowl, and shake on the walnut oil. Toss. Serve immediately, garnishing with walnuts if you like.

Serves 1 to 2.

Sort of Grad's Father's Dandelion Salad

Linda Gradishar, a.k.a. Grad, and I have never met. We have bonded on the internet over shared loves such as books (she writes a literary blog called "The Curious Reader") and the lyrics of Johnny Mercer. Mercer lived in Grad's hometown of Savannah, Georgia.

When Grad learned that I was playing with dandelion greens, she wrote to me: "OMG. You've touched on one of my fondest childhood memories of my father gathering wild dandelion greens every spring and then family members coming to the house to get their share. He made it with boiled eggs, bacon, and a bacon-vinegar dressing. He'd insist, 'You gotta eat it while it's warm.' We looked forward to it every year. We waited for the dandelion salad … it didn't wait for us." Grad doesn't have her father's recipe so I'm not sure I made the salad correctly, but what I made tasted pretty darn good!

4 strips thick bacon
4 cups dandelion greens, rinsed and drained
3 tablespoons cider vinegar
2 tablespoons water
1 tablespoon sugar
freshly ground pepper to taste
8 tiny red potatoes, cooked
2 hard-boiled eggs, chopped
a few thin strips of red onion

Fry the bacon in a skillet. Remove the bacon and crumble it. Place the greens in a heatproof bowl. In the skillet, add the vinegar, the water, and the sugar to the warm bacon fat. Stir over very low heat until the sugar melts; then add the pepper and toss the warm liquid over the greens. Add the potatoes, the egg pieces, and the onion strips, and toss again. Serve immediately. Serves 4.

Taffy's Asparagus Penne

My family served this to my mother Jan (a.k.a. Taffy because she liked to swim in salt water) for Mother's Day one year. It has become a May staple for us.

1 pound penne
2 pounds fresh asparagus, washed, trimmed, and cut into bite-size pieces
1/2 cup extra-virgin olive oil (plus a bit more if you like)
10 large cloves of garlic, cut lengthwise into thin pieces
1/2 teaspoon salt (optional; if you put lots of salt in the penne and asparagus waters you won't need it)
freshly ground pepper to taste
1/4 cup (1/2 stick) sweet butter
1/2 pound Prosciutto, thinly sliced and then shredded (optional)
freshly grated Italian cheese (such as Parmesan or Pecorino Romano) to taste—at least 1 cup, and maybe more
1 handful fresh parsley, finely chopped

First, cook the penne according to the package instructions. When it is cooked *al dente* drain it, rinse it in cold water to cool it off, and drain it again.

While the pasta is cooking, place the asparagus in boiling water, and boil for 2 minutes. Carefully drain the asparagus, rinse it with very cold water, and drain it again.

When the pasta is ready and drained, pour the oil into a large skillet, and warm it over medium heat for about a minute, until it begins to shimmer. The oil will be very hot. Carefully add the pieces of garlic to the oil and cook, stirring vigorously, until the garlic begins to brown. (This won't take long.)

Add the asparagus, the salt (if needed), and the pepper to the garlic. Cook for another 2 minutes, shaking or stirring gently. Add the pasta and the butter and cook until the vegetables and pasta are hot and well mixed, 3 to 4 minutes. Turn off the heat, and toss in the Prosciutto if you want to use it.

Carefully transfer the mixture to a serving bowl, and toss in lots of cheese. Sprinkle the chopped parsley on top. Serve to your mother and other guests immediately. Serves 8.

Tinky's Asparagus Fritters

I admit it; I can find ways to make even the healthiest fruits and vegetables fattening! Like the penne and the dandelion salad above, this is a once-a-year (at most) treat. But, golly, is it good.

1 pound asparagus
2 cups flour, divided
1 teaspoon baking powder
1 teaspoon salt
freshly ground pepper to taste
2 teaspoons lemon zest
1/2 cup freshly grated Parmesan cheese
1 cup beer
1 egg
peanut or canola oil as needed for frying
lemon wedges
coarse salt (optional)

Preheat the oven to 200 degrees.

Wash and trim the asparagus spears, and cut them into small pieces—between 1 and 2 inches long. Pop the pieces of asparagus into boiling water. Return the water to the boil, and cook the asparagus for 1 more minute. Drain the pieces in a colander with ice so that they will stop cooking immediately.

In a bowl thoroughly combine 1 cup of the flour, the baking powder, the salt, the pepper, the lemon zest, and the cheese.

Whisk together the beer and the egg. Stir this liquid mixture into the flour mixture. (A few lumps are just fine.) Place the remaining cup of flour in a small bowl.

Pour the oil into a frying pan until it is about 1 inch deep. Heat the oil until it is about 350 degrees.

Dredge each piece of asparagus in the small bowl of flour; then dip it into the liquid fritter batter so that it is coated.

Pop each fritter into the oil and cook it quickly, turning as needed, until it is golden brown. Do not crowd the fritters in the pan. (Don't worry if the flour and batter don't adhere perfectly to the asparagus spears. A little green peeking out of the batter looks attractive. And don't worry if your fritters are oddly shaped. Each one will have its own personality, and that will be just fine.)

When individual fritters are ready drain them on paper towels and store them in the warm oven until all of the fritters have been cooked. You may end up with a little extra asparagus if you run out of batter or just get tired of cooking. Use this in a salad or a stir fry.

Serve with lemon wedges so that your guests can sprinkle a little juice on their fritters. Diners may add a little coarse salt for extra zing if they wish. Serves 4 to 6.

Beds of Rhubarb, Forest Trees etc. on grounds of The Gardner Nursery Company, Osage, Iowa.

Pies and Tarts

Rhubarb Country

I write this as rhubarb is in full swing in my corner of western Massachusetts, pushing up outrageously large leaves to protect its red and green stalks. I love living in rhubarb country.

Areas like ours with a relatively cool climate are ideal for rhubarb, which must have temperatures below 40 degrees Fahrenheit at some point during the year in order to grow. It is cultivated extensively in the northern United States, in Canada, and in Europe and England. Rhubarb plants are hardy and don't need a lot of care.

Obviously, we New Englanders are not the only people enjoying rhubarb right now. A quick internet search yields word of rhubarb festivals in a variety of places. I wish I could go to every single one of them. Instead, I'm mentioning just a few here in case readers feel like a spot of travel.

Of course, the annual rhubarb celebration in Yorkshire in February, mentioned in my discussion of "forcing rhubarb," is the first festival of the calendar year. In addition to wonderful-sounding rhubarb meals, the festival recently included tastings of rhubarb cheese made by a local cheese monger, Cryer & Stott. It is named Ruby Gold.

The United States has plenty of rhubarb celebrations as well. Lanesboro, Minnesota, calls itself the Rhubarb Capital of its state. Its annual rhubarb festival takes place in June. It features rhubarb games known as the Rhubarb Olympics. These include rhubarb golf, in which participants use a stalk of rhubarb to propel balls into the air. The festival also sponsors a cooking contest, as well as a Rhubarb Rant Speakers Corner for people who love to spout off about this controversial plant. Best of all (to me), it is launched every year by the singing of the "Rhubarb National Anthem" by a group called the Rhubarb Sisters.

If I were a little closer, I would ask to join this singing group. Meanwhile, I relate as a sister from afar.

The annual Rhubarb Fest in Kitchen Kettle Village in Intercourse, Pennsylvania, includes a dance called the Rhubarb Stroll and an automobile Rhubarb Derby.

Aledo, Illinois, also joins in the fun. Its festival includes sales by local businesses, myriad rhubarb pies, and a contest to see who can grow the largest rhubarb leaf.

Conrad, Montana, celebrates rhubarb in conjunction with something called "Whoop-Up Days." The festivities include a car show and a rodeo.

Sumner, Washington, bills itself as the "rhubarb pie capital of the world." Sumner celebrates both summer Rhubarb Days and a fall Rhubarb Pie Festival.

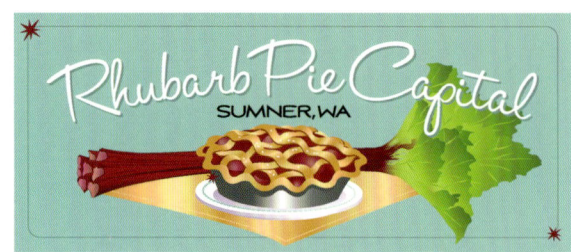

L & S Gardens, a nursery in La Pine, Oregon, sponsors a rhubarb festival for the community. There co-owner Linda Stephenson features vendors, live music, and of course rhubarb—much of it prepared in various forms by the local Dutch Oven Cooking Club, of which Linda is president.

She and her husband Sonny became interested in using cast-iron Dutch ovens outdoors after reading about Sonny's great-grandmother's cooking practices in an old family diary.

The nursery also sells fresh rhubarb and rhubarb plants that day, as well as a small cookbook Linda has written, appropriately titled *Rhubarb Country*.

Nearer to my home, Lenox, Massachusetts, has been celebrating rhubarb on a Saturday in June since 2013.

Many other rhubarb festivals may be found in the U.S., from Connecticut to Washington State. Several take place yearly in Canada as well. Someday I hope to visit them all—with this book in hand, of course! Meanwhile, I will celebrate rhubarb at home with pies and tarts.

Love, Laughter, and Rhubarb

Pie Starts with Crust

Every time I make pie I think of my late mother. Taffy had many wonderful qualities. She was smart. She was brave. She was funny. She was loyal.

She was also the proverbial dab hand at pastry. Her Vermont mother and grandmother taught her to mix and roll out pie crust at an early age.

She passed many of her culinary skills on to me … but not her pie proficiency. It was only after her death that I realized that she had always been our family's designated pie-crust roller and that it was time for me to step up to the pie plate.

As I write this six years after her death, I can roll out pastry for pie reasonably efficiently. I'm not sure I'll ever match the skill my mother and grandmother exhibited. They baked pies regularly; I bake them occasionally.

I would be remiss, however, if I didn't include at least a few pie recipes in this book. Rhubarb is often referred to as "pie plant" for a reason: pie is the first, if not the only, dish many Americans think to make with it. Here, then, are a few rhubarbarian ideas for pie lovers.

Pie begins with crust. Estelle Cade, whose mother's recipe appears below, recalls that her mother used lard to make crust. One of my favorite bakers in the world, Doris Lewis of Florida, Massachusetts, still prefers lard in her pie crusts. Doris swears that lard makes the flakiest crusts—and Doris makes a lot of pies.

I had a bad experience with lard, however. Doris generously gave me some of the lard she buys in bulk, and I attempted to make Estelle's mother's pie. The crust was flaky. Unfortunately, the lard had gone bad, and the pie tasted rancid. This wasn't Doris's fault; the expiration date on the lard container was still well in the future. But that crust did deter me from working with lard after that. I'm a coward!

Below is my go-to non-lard crust recipe. As most bakers know, shortening makes flakier crusts, and butter makes tastier ones. As I write this, I am still perfecting my butter-crust skills. So I'm sharing my shortening recipe. I hope my next book will contain a fool-proof butter-crust recipe. Until that day, please use this crust, which tastes delicious. (Any crust you make at home is bound to taste better than one you buy.)

Bob Stone's Fullerville Pie Crust

My late neighbor Bob Stone gave me this recipe. He swore that the egg and the vinegar made his crust easy to handle, and I find that they definitely help the novice pie maker. I included the recipe last fall when I taught a pre-Thanksgiving pie class at the Baker's Pin in Northampton, Massachusetts. My students all told me at the beginning of the class that they were nervous about rolling out pie crust. By the end of the evening, they all felt fairly confident with a rolling pin. They had absorbed my pie mantra: "Show no fear!"

Bob's recipe makes a lot of crust. If you need to make only one pie, you can either try to divide an egg in half (hint: beat it first!) or freeze crust for a future occasion.

Fullerville, by the way, is the name of a section of my hometown of Hawley, Massachusetts, in which Bob lived for many years.

4 cups flour
1 teaspoon salt
1–3/4 cups shortening
1/2 cup ice water plus a bit more if needed
1 tablespoon white vinegar (cider vinegar works as well)
1 egg

Combine the flour and the salt in a bowl. Cut in the shortening, using a pastry blender or two knives, until it is crumbly. Do not over mix. Whisk together the water, the vinegar, and the egg, and stir them gently into the flour mixture. If the dough seems too dry (this is rare), add a tiny bit more cold water.

Roll the dough into four circles. Makes enough crust for 2 double 9-inch pies.

Coconut-Rhubarb Pie

It took me a while to get the proportions right in this recipe, but it's a definite keeper. The coconut flavor dominates, but the rhubarb peeks out here and there, both physically (making pretty little rubies in your pie) and taste wise.

1 single 9-inch pie crust
6 tablespoons (3/4 stick) sweet butter
2 eggs plus 1 yolk, beaten
1 teaspoon vanilla
1 cup sugar
3/4 cup sweetened flaked coconut
1 cup finely chopped rhubarb

Preheat the oven to 350 degrees. Place the crust in a pie pan. Let it sit in the refrigerator while you prepare the pie filling.

Melt the butter and let it cool for a few minutes. In a bowl combine the eggs, the vanilla, and the sugar; then whisk in the melted butter, followed by the coconut.

Take the pie crust out of the refrigerator, and sprinkle the rhubarb around the bottom. Spoon the coconut filling on top.

Bake the pie until the crust is brown and the filling is set, about 40 minutes. Cool to room temperature before serving. Makes 6 to 8 servings.

Estelle (left), her mother, and Estelle's daughter Prudy in 1951.

Mom's Rhubarb Pie

Estelle Cade is a lively senior in my area who contributes to a writing group that collects memories. The pie she mentions in the passage below sounds a little different from the recipe she gave me—but my neighbors certainly enjoyed eating the version I baked. Here's a bit of Estelle's take on pie, reprinted with my thanks to her:

I grew up with Dad's bounteous rhubarb patch in our back yard, there for the picking, all we'd ever want and more, and Mom canned numerous jars for our enjoyment during the winter. Mom's rhubarb pie was an eagerly anticipated dessert at family dinners; a flaky crust (made with lard, naturally) covering a filling of juicy rhubarb and sugar, thickened slightly with a bit of flour and a pat of butter—just the best, always, usually accompanied by a delicious wedge of really sharp New England cheese—the perfect finishing touch. Another choice might be a small side dish of stewed, sweetened rhubarb (rhubarb sauce) to accompany some juicy pork chops—a taste like no other.

enough dough for 1 double 8-inch pie crust
3 cups rhubarb
2 eggs
1 cup sugar
1/2 teaspoon salt
2 tablespoons flour

Preheat the oven to 425 degrees. Separate the pastry into two rounds, and roll them out. Place one in the bottom of an 8-inch pie plate.

Arrange the rhubarb on top of that crust. In a bowl, whisk together the remaining ingredients for the filling, and pour them over the rhubarb. Place the top crust over all, and crimp the edges. Make holes in the top of the pie so it can breathe.

Bake the pie for 5 to 10 minutes (don't let the crust get too dark); then reduce the heat to 350 degrees and bake for another 40 minutes or until the crust is golden brown and the filling begins to bubble up through the holes. Makes 6 servings.

Rustic Rhubarb Tart

If you're not comfortable rolling out pie crust, you'll like this recipe. It uses a simple, slightly sweet dough patted out with the hands rather than a rolling pin. I confess: "rustic" is a code word for messy. This mess ends up looking very pretty. It also tastes terrific.

1-1/4 cups flour
1/2 cup sugar, divided
1/2 teaspoon salt
1/2 cup (1 stick) cold sweet butter
1 egg yolk
ice water as needed
2 cups chopped rhubarb
1 teaspoon cinnamon

In a cold bowl combine the flour, 1/4 cup of the sugar, and the salt. Carefully cut in the butter, leaving some lumps.

Whisk together the egg yolk and 3 tablespoons of ice water. Use a fork to stir them into the butter mixture. Add a little more cold water as needed until the dough is capable of being formed into a ball (but barely). Wrap the ball of dough in wax paper and refrigerate it for at least 1 hour.

At the end of the hour, preheat the oven to 400 degrees. Line a cookie sheet that has edges that come up the sides (so nothing can spill into your oven) with silicone or parchment.

Pat the dough into a circle about 9 inches in diameter on the pan. Return the patted-out dough on its pan to the refrigerator while you prepare the rhubarb.

Toss the rhubarb pieces into the cinnamon and the remaining sugar. Arrange the tossed pieces on your crust. You may have trouble fitting them all into the space; do your best.

Bake until the crust browns nicely (it's best a little crispy), about 20 to 30 minutes. Your tart will probably ooze a little butter, which it will mostly reabsorb if you let it cool for a few minutes before serving it. If the tart looks as though it is browning too fast, reduce the heat to 300 degrees. Serves 8.

Nantucket Rhubarb Pie

It took me a while to make up my mind whether to include this recipe here. It's based on a popular cranberry recipe. As I have mentioned before, I tend to think of cranberries as the autumnal version of rhubarb.

Nantucket Cranberry Pie isn't actually a pie, more a cross between a cookie and a cake. I think it's called a pie because it's baked in a pie pan—but I really have no idea. I just know that it tastes great and comes together in no time at all. I don't need more information than that.

When one makes the pie with cranberries, those little red gems rise toward the top of the pie and make pretty bumps on the surface. Rhubarb is wetter and therefore denser than cranberries so it doesn't actually rise. Consequently, the rhubarb version of the pie is less attractive than its fall cousin. Taste always trumps appearance for me, however, so I decided to give readers the opportunity to try this delectable combination of sweet and tart.

2 cups relatively finely chopped rhubarb
1-1/2 cups sugar
3/4 cup (1-1/2 sticks) sweet butter, melted and then allowed to sit for a few minutes to cool
2 eggs, beaten
1 cup flour
1 teaspoon vanilla extract

Generously grease a 9-inch nonreactive pie pan. Preheat the oven to 375 degrees. Place the pieces of rhubarb in the bottom of the pan. Sprinkle 1/2 cup of the sugar on top. Make a batter of the remaining ingredients, first combining the butter and the remaining sugar and then adding the eggs, the flour, and the vanilla. Pour the batter over the rhubarb.

Bake for 35 to 40 minutes. Top with whipped cream. (Ice cream works well, too. Or just serve it alone.) Serves 8.

Strawberry-Rhubarb Cream-Cheese Tart

This recipe has a lot of steps, but none of them is hard! I do most of the work a day ahead and assemble the tart the next day. This is a very full tart and a very rich, sweet one. In fact, a friend from Amherst, Massachusetts, Bernie Rubinstein, blanched when he saw this recipe. "Cream cheese AND condensed milk, Tinky?" he queried in a disapproving tone. No one who ate it complained, however.

for the crust:
1 stick butter, softened
1/3 cup granulated sugar
1-1/3 cups all-purpose flour
1/3 teaspoon salt
1 egg yolk
1 teaspoon vanilla

for the filling:
1 8-ounce package cream cheese, at room temperature
1 14-ounce can sweetened condensed milk
1 teaspoon vanilla
1/4 cup key-lime juice

for the topping:
2 cups sliced rhubarb
1 tablespoon key-lime juice
1/2 cup sugar
2 tablespoons cornstarch
2 cups halved strawberries

Begin with the crust. Preheat the oven to 350 degrees. In a mixing bowl, cream together the butter and the sugar until they are just blended. Add the flour and the salt, and stir until the mixture seems crumbly. (It will be dry.)

In a small bowl whisk together the egg yolk and the vanilla; drizzle them over the flour mixture. Combine until the flour mixture is evenly moist; it will still be crumbly.

Place the dough in a greased 9-inch tart pan. Press the dough evenly over the bottom and up the sides of pan. Prick the bottom of the crust to keep it from puffing up too much.

Put the crust in the freezer, uncovered, while you preheat the oven to 375 degrees.

Bake the crust for 16 to 20 minutes or until it is golden brown. Check it after 15 minutes; if it seems to be rising up too much, gently depress it with a fork, and continue baking. Cool the crust completely.

Next, make the filling. Beat the cream cheese until it is soft; then beat in the condensed milk, the vanilla, and the key-lime juice.

Spoon this mixture over the cooled crust, and refrigerate for several hours. (Overnight is best; you want to make sure that the filling is firm enough.)

Finally, make the topping. In a heavy, nonreactive saucepan combine the rhubarb, the lime juice, the sugar, and the cornstarch. Let this mixture sit for 1 hour to juice up.

Bring the rhubarb mixture to a boil over medium-low heat, and boil gently until it thickens, stirring constantly. (This won't take more than a few minutes.) Remove it from the heat and let it sit for 5 minutes. Stir in the strawberries.

Refrigerate this topping until it is cool; then spoon it over the pie filling. Refrigerate the pie until you are ready to serve it. Serves 8.

Rhubarb, Rhubarb, Rhubarb!

A Meaningful Word

As I approach the plethora of sweets still to come in this book I'd like to explore the word "rhubarb." My friend Peter asked me whether rhubarb didn't have more than one meaning. I did a little research—and was he ever right! When you've said rhubarb, you've said a mouthful in more ways than one.

Other foods may enjoy one or two definitions beyond their edible ones. A peach is a pretty girl, and something peachy is just swell. We blow a raspberry to show disrespect. And spinach can mean "humbug" as part of the English phrase "gammon and spinach" or all by itself, as in the immortal Irving Berlin lyric, "I say it's spinach and the hell with it!"

Rhubarb, however, has so much personality that its figurative uses may almost rival its culinary ones in number.

First of all, of course, rhubarb is a reddish, stringy plant that originated in China. People either love or hate its strong, tart flavor. (I'm in the love camp, as you may have guessed.)

The genesis of the word "rhubarb" comes from its presence along the banks of the Volga River in Siberia; it is a combination of "Rha" (the Greek word for the Volga) and the word "barbarum," or barbarian. (Obviously those who named the plant were less than enthusiastic about it. I don't find it at all barbaric.)

Beyond its culinary meaning, rhubarb is a theatrical phrase used by actors in crowd scenes. In Shakespeare's day and beyond, extras onstage would intone "rhubarb, rhubarb, rhubarb" to simulate muttering, particularly angry muttering.

I like to think that the peasants coming after the monster with torches in the classic film *Frankenstein* used the phrase, although I have no proof that they did.

Perhaps because of its slightly harsh syllables, rhubarb also connotes a fight, usually a spirited one. In the mid-20th century the word became attached to baseball. It was used most famously by colorful sportscaster Red Barber to describe an altercation on the field—between teams, between players and umpires, or between players and fans. Barber called Ebbets Field, home of the Brooklyn Dodgers, "the rhubarb patch." Apparently, the Dodgers had a strong, tart flavor.

According to the Oxford English Dictionary, rhubarb is sometimes used to mean "nonsense." (Perhaps Irving Berlin should have written, "I say it's RHUBARB and the hell with it!")

The word also describes low-level aircraft strafing in time of war (at least it did during World War II). And it was used centuries ago as an adjective to mean bitter or tart. The OED also lists related words, including "rhubarber," which refers to an actor milling around in a crowd scene.

In case I haven't provided enough meanings of the word for you, the *Keene Sentinel* offered several more in a 2000 article titled "The Hidden Life of Rhubarb."

I asked its author, John Fladd, where he discovered so many rhubarb usages. He referred me to Eric Partridge's *Dictionary of Slang and Unconventional English*. Partridge found myriad meanings for rhubarb.

In the 19th century the word was used vulgarly to refer to the genital region, as in the expression (unfamiliar to me), "How's your rhubarb coming up, Bill?"

It has also stood in for a loan, a bill for payment, an advance on one's wages, and a rural area (as a synonym for "the Sticks"). I guess I live in the Rhubarbs.

Finally, Fladd (citing Partridge) noted, "There is a Canadian phrase, 'hitting the rhubarb,' that means running one's car off the road — 'You'd better not have another drink, Stanley, or you'll hit the rhubarb.'"

Before I hit the rhubarb myself, I guess I should get to some more recipes. In this chapter I address wet (and sort of wet) rhubarb dishes. I know that "wet" isn't a very descriptive word—but it's apt. Here this catch-all term refers to rhubarb desserts that need to be served in a bowl.

Stewed Rhubarb

My family and neighbors were very patient during the testing of recipes for this book, facing and eating rhubarb in many, many forms. One day, however, my brother had had enough. "Couldn't we just have some stewed rhubarb?" he begged. David, this recipe is for you. It's the basic rhubarb that made its appearance frequently at our grandmother's oval dining-room table in Rutland, Vermont. That table may now be found in my kitchen. So, frequently, may the stewed rhubarb. The cinnamon is a tradition in our family; if you want more concentrated rhubarb flavor, omit it.

1 pound rhubarb (about 3 cups chopped)
1/2 cup sugar
1 teaspoon lemon juice
1 teaspoon cinnamon (optional)

Wash and trim the rhubarb. Cut it into 1-inch pieces. In a heavy, nonreactive saucepan, combine all the ingredients and cover. Let the pan sit for an hour or so to allow the rhubarb to juice up; then cook over low heat for 5 to 7 minutes. Keep an eye on the pot to avoid messy boiling over. Serve plain or add cream or ice cream. Serves 4. This recipe may be multiplied.

Strawberry-Rhubarb Trifle

After I made my rhubarb cordial (see page 23), I pondered how to use it. Of course, one could drink it in small quantities as an after-dinner liqueur. One could add it to fruit salad, and I have. But I wanted something special. And then I thought of trifle!

This recipe uses strawberries as well as rhubarb—both in the jam, to brighten the taste, and optionally in the topping. If you use the strawberries for the topping (you don't have to, but they're awfully tasty), be sure to use up your trifle as quickly as possible. The strawberries tend to liquefy.

for the base:
ladyfingers (9 to 12, depending on the shape of your serving dish)
1/2 cup strawberry jam
3/8 cup (6 tablespoons) rhubarb cordial (see page 23)

for the custard:
3/4 cup milk
1/2 cup heavy cream
2 tablespoons sugar
2 eggs plus 1 yolk, well beaten
1 teaspoon vanilla

for the topping:
1 cup whipped cream
1 cup lightly sweetened strawberries (optional)

Split the ladyfingers and spread them with half of the jam. Arrange them on the bottom and sides of a 1-quart bowl, jam side up. Drip the cordial on the lady fingers and allow it to soak in while you make the custard.

Heat the milk and the cream in the top of a double boiler until warm to the touch. Add the sugar to the eggs. Pour the heated milk/cream onto the eggs, and return the liquid to the double boiler. Stir it over medium-low heat until it is thick, but do not boil it. Add the vanilla. Pour the custard on top of the ladyfingers. Let it cool and set it until firm in the refrigerator.

When the custard has set, add another thin layer of jam, and cover the whole with the whipped cream. Decorate with the strawberries, if you like, added immediately before serving. Serves 4 to 6.

Rhubarb Chantilly

This pudding-like recipe was given to me by a former schoolmate, Rose Franke Koch, who has been making it for almost 50 years. Rose's original recipe suggests cooking the rhubarb and sugar in the top of a double boiler, but I found that that took forever. (Actually, I don't know how long it really took because I gave up after half an hour of cooking. The rhubarb had generated a lot of liquid but hadn't gotten at all tender!) I went with a basic rhubarb puree. I hope Rose will forgive me.

6 cups chopped rhubarb
2 cups sugar
2 cups heavy cream
1 teaspoon vanilla

Combine the rhubarb and the sugar in a nonreactive saucepan. Let them sit, covered, for an hour or so to allow the rhubarb to begin to juice up.

Gently cook the combination until the rhubarb is just tender, stirring from time to time. (You don't want it to break down completely.)

Remove the rhubarb mixture from the heat, and let it cool to room temperature.

Whip the cream until it is stiff. Beat in the vanilla; then fold in the rhubarb mixture. Spoon the chantilly into a bowl and chill it for at least 6 hours. Serves 6.

Rhubarb-Apple Crisp

We still have a few apples in our area when rhubarb season arrives—and one does occasionally get to pick fall rhubarb (if the season is just right!). So this tasty combination can be accomplished.

2 cups chopped rhubarb
3 cups sliced apples (core but don't bother to peel unless you're fussy, and use a fairly sturdy apple)
1/2 cup white sugar plus 1/2 cup later
2 pinches salt
the juice of 1/2 lemon
1/2 cup flour
1/2 cup firmly packed brown sugar
1/2 cup oats (regular, not steel cut or quick)
1 teaspoon cinnamon
1/2 cup (1 stick) sweet butter

Preheat the oven to 350 degrees. In a bowl toss together the rhubarb, the apples, 1/2 cup sugar, the first pinch of salt, and the lemon juice. Spread them in the bottom of a buttered 2-quart baking dish.

In a small bowl combine the flour, the remaining white sugar, the brown sugar, the oats, the cinnamon, and the second pinch of salt. Cut or rub in the butter until you have coarse crumbs. I prefer to rub it in since I'm a tactile cook. Gently spread this combination over the fruit mixture. (It will be a little messy!)

Bake the crisp until it is brown and bubbly, at least 30 to 40 minutes. Serve with the topping of your choice—cream, whipped cream, ice cream, or frozen yogurt. Serves 6.

Susan Shauger's Rhubarb Cobbler

This recipe comes from a retired teacher and semi-retired attorney named Susan Shauger who sings in my church choir. For some reason, I had never made a cobbler before Susan gave me her recipe. Now I make cobblers with just about any fruit—sour cherries, blueberries, peaches, and so forth. The Food Timeline calls cobblers "an amalgam of European tradition and American ingenuity." Historian Lynne Oliver adds that the idea of a cobbler—basically, biscuit dough on top of fruit—probably originated in the American west, where stovetop cooking made pies difficult.

As for the term "cobbler," my friend Michael Collins argues that perhaps the name comes from the roughness of the top of a fruit cobbler, which might evoke cobblestones. I would argue that it might come from the process of cobbling the dish together. In any case, it's a simple, tasty dessert.

for the rhubarb base:
3/4 cup sugar
2 tablespoons cornstarch
4 cups chopped rhubarb
2 tablespoons lemon juice
1 teaspoon cinnamon
1 tablespoon butter, diced

for the cobbler crust:
1 cup flour
2 tablespoons sugar
1-1/2 teaspoons baking powder
1/4 teaspoon salt
1/4 cup (1/2 stick) butter
1/4 cup milk
1 egg, beaten

for the topping:
2 tablespoons brown sugar

Combine the sugar and the cornstarch for the base in a medium nonreactive pot. Stir in the rhubarb and the lemon juice. Cover this mixture and let it sit for an hour or two.

Preheat the oven to 400 degrees. Butter a 1-1/2-quart casserole dish.

Uncover the rhubarb mixture and bring it to a boil, stirring occasionally. Boil, stirring gently, for 1 minute. Remove the fruit from the heat and stir in the cinnamon.

Spread the rhubarb mixture in the prepared pan. Dot the top with butter.

To make the crust, whisk together the flour, the sugar, the baking powder, and the salt. Cut in the butter, but don't overdo. You should still see tiny pieces of butter.

Whisk together the milk and the egg. Add them to the dry ingredients, and mix just until moist. Drop this mixture onto the rhubarb, and spread it around to cover the fruit. Sprinkle clumps of brown sugar over all.

Bake until lightly browned, 20 to 25 minutes. Serves 8.

Miss Ginny's Rhubarb Crumble

A crumble is a wonderful thing—lighter than a crisp, easier than a pie. It's the perfect dessert to make when you learn at 6 p.m. that dinner guests are expected at 7. This recipe comes from my friend and fellow journalist Virginia Ray. Ginny says, "I love the sweet/sourness of this crumble, which reminds me of picking rhubarb at my little farm in Pennsylvania, right from the garden, and transforming the bitterness to yummy-ness!"

I love it just the way it is—but if you want to get adventurous you can add a little orange peel to the rhubarb/sugar mixture and/or a little crystallized ginger to the topping. Ginny originally used all flour in the topping; I put in some oats for extra nutrition and crunch.

2 pounds rhubarb (6 cups), cut into 1-inch pieces
1/4 cup sugar (Ginny likes this organic; I have been known to substitute 3 tablespoons of honey from my friends at Warm Colors Apiary)
1/2 teaspoon cinnamon
1/2 cup flour
1/4 cup oats (traditional, not quick cooking or steel cut)
1/4 cup (1/2 stick) salted butter
1/2 cup brown sugar

Preheat the oven to 400 degrees. Place the rhubarb in a buttered, nonreactive pie dish.

Sprinkle on the sugar and cinnamon. Place the flour and the oats in a bowl. Add the butter and cut it in with knives or a pastry blender. (Your hands will do in a pinch.) Add the brown sugar and mix again until crumbly.

Sprinkle this mixture evenly over the rhubarb, pressing down lightly. Bake for 30 minutes or until golden brown and crisp. Serves 6 to 8.

DIVIDING AND REPLANTING RHUBARB

Rhubarb Sorbet

I received mixed reviews for this sorbet, adapted from a recipe in The New York Times. *Don't get me wrong; everyone liked it and consumed it. Adults tended to feel that the cinnamon obscured the flavor of the rhubarb. Children viewed the cinnamon as essential. I guess I'm a child at heart.*

1 pound rhubarb (about 3 cups), chopped
1 cup sugar
1 pinch salt
3 tablespoons key-lime juice
1 cup water
1/2 teaspoon cinnamon

Combine the rhubarb, the sugar, the salt, and the lime juice in a nonreactive saucepan. Add the water, bring the mixture to a boil, reduce the heat, and simmer until the rhubarb softens (8 to 10 minutes). Just before turning off the heat, stir in the cinnamon.

Puree the rhubarb mixture with a blender or immersion blender until it is relatively smooth. Cool it to room temperature; then chill it in the refrigerator for a few hours or up to a day.

Use an ice-cream maker to churn the sorbet until it is frozen. Transfer the sorbet to an airtight container and chill it for at least an hour before serving. Serves 4 to 6.

About Baked Hawley

One year my friend Peter Beck asked me to make Baked Alaska for his birthday. I was thrilled.

Like Cherries Jubilee or Bananas Foster, Baked Alaska is a showy dessert associated with "fancy" mid-20th-century restaurants.

I pictured myself whipping it up casually in a little hostess apron, looking like Barbara Stanwyck and throwing my dinner guests into paroxysms of joy.

By the time I had finished putting all the pieces together I was a little too messy (and a little too me) to resemble Miss Stanwyck. My guests were pretty joyful, however.

For readers unfamiliar with Baked Alaska, here is a bit of history. It's a dish I would never have thought of on my own so its background fascinates me.

Cooks of many nationalities (including the Chinese, who probably invented ice cream, and the cook in Thomas Jefferson's kitchen) experimented with insulating ice cream with pastry and then baking it.

It was apparently the American-born chemist Benjamin Thompson who originated the exact formula for Baked Alaska in 1804. Fiercely loyal to the British in the Revolutionary War (he spied for them), Thompson spent his life after the war in Europe. He was named a count of the Holy Roman Empire by the elector of Bavaria for his social-reform work there. Thompson chose the title Count Rumford because of his fondness for the town of Concord, New Hampshire, originally known as Rumford.

Count Rumford is best known for creating the kitchen range (known as the Rumford Range or Stove), which revolutionized cooking by giving home and restaurant cooks an alternative to hard-to-control and wasteful open fires.

In 1804, while experimenting with the insulating power of egg whites, he invented the dish we call Baked Alaska. He called it omelette surprise. His surprise was cake topped with ice cream and meringue and then browned in the oven. The name Baked Alaska came later, many say from Chef Charles Ranhofer at Delmonico's Restaurant in New York, in honor of the 1867 purchase of the Alaska territory.

In his cookbook *The Epicurean*, Ranhofer himself called the dish Alaska, Florida, to celebrate its juxtaposition of hot and cold. It was first called Baked Alaska in print by Fannie Farmer, the original author of the basic cookbook (my favorite!) that bears her name.

With rhubarb on my mind as always, I decided that Peter's Baked Alaska would be no ordinary Alaska but a Baked Hawley, featuring one of the most copious crops in my hometown of Hawley, Massachusetts (yes, rhubarb).

This 1800 cartoon from the Library of Congress depicts Count Rumford.

I called Gary Schafer and Barbara Fingold, who for many years owned Bart's and Snow's Ice Cream in Greenfield, Massachusetts. I figured if anyone could tell me how to make rhubarb ice cream it would be they. Bart's ice cream is always delicious and tastes homemade.

Barbara and Gary suggested that I wait until the very end of the freezing process to add the rhubarb so that its liquid didn't interfere with the consistency of my ice cream.

Of course, you don't HAVE to use rhubarb ice cream. You don't even have to use homemade ice cream. Many Baked Alaska recipes ensure super insulation of the ice cream by refreezing it, along with the cake below, for several hours before putting the meringue on top and baking the dish. If you want to try that method, you'll be better off with commercial ice cream since homemade ice cream is best eaten fresh.

You may also vary this recipe. It can easily be made bigger or given a change of flavors. A brownie base with peppermint-stick ice cream could be Baked Noël. Peach ice cream could be Baked Georgia. Apple cake in autumn could serve as the base for Baked Back to School. (Baked Teacher doesn't sound friendly.) And so on.

We all loved the rhubarb version.

I know this seems like a long recipe. It's not hard; it just has quite a few steps.

Baked Hawley

for the rhubarb ice cream (which has three parts, the rhubarb puree, the custard, and the final custard ingredients):

the puree:
2 cups finely chopped rhubarb
1/4 cup plus 2 tablespoons sugar
1 pinch salt
1 tablespoon lemon juice

the custard:
3/4 cup milk
2 egg yolks (save the whites for the meringue!)
1/3 cup sugar

the final custard ingredients:
3/4 cup heavy cream
1 teaspoon vanilla
1 pinch salt (for the custard)

for the cake:
1/4 cup (1/2 stick) sweet butter at room temperature
1/2 cup sugar
1 egg, separated
1 teaspoon baking powder
1 pinch salt
3/4 cup flour
1/4 cup milk
1/2 teaspoon vanilla

for the meringue:
2 egg whites
1 pinch cream of tartar
1/4 cup sugar

The day before you want to make your dessert, start by making the rhubarb puree. Combine the rhubarb, its sugar, its salt, and the lemon juice in a small nonreactive saucepan. Let them sit for an hour or so.

When the mixture has juiced up, stir it and bring it to a boil. Simmer it, stirring frequently, until the rhubarb is soft and most of the liquid has boiled off. Set it aside to cool; then refrigerate it. Move on to the custard.

In a small-to-medium saucepan, heat the milk until it steams but does not boil. Meanwhile, in a bowl whisk the egg yolks and the 1/3 cup sugar until they thicken and turn light yellow (about 4 minutes). Refrigerate the egg whites to use later in the meringue.

Whisk a little hot milk into the sweet egg yolks; then whisk in a little more. Repeat this process; then whisk the egg-yolk mixture into the hot milk. Heat over medium heat, whisking constantly, until the custard begins to thicken but does not boil. Strain the custard through a strainer into a heat-proof bowl. Cool it to room temperature; then refrigerate it for several hours or preferably overnight.

Later or the next day, make the cake. Preheat the oven to 350 degrees, and grease and flour a 7-inch-round cake pan.

Cream the butter, and beat in the sugar. Beat in the egg yolk, reserving the white. Stir in the baking powder and the salt. Gently add the flour and the milk alternately, beginning and ending with the flour. Stir in the vanilla.

Peter contemplates Baked Hawley.

Using a clean bowl and beater, whip the egg white until it forms stiff peaks. Fold it into the cake batter, and spoon the batter into the prepared pan. Bake until a toothpick inserted into the center comes out clean (about 30 minutes). Let the cake rest for 10 minutes before removing it from the pan. Let it cool.

About 1/2 hour before you are ready to make the Baked Hawley, preheat the oven to 450 degrees, and get out the custard. Add the cream, the vanilla, and the salt, and pour all into an ice-cream maker. Start churning. Bring the 2 egg whites to room temperature.

When the ice cream is done, add the rhubarb puree to it. Churn briefly.

Rinse a wooden board on both sides with cold water, and shake it dry. Cut out a round of brown paper slightly larger than the cake in diameter. Place it on the wooden board.

Using an electric mixer, beat the egg whites and cream of tartar until they begin to stiffen. Slowly add the sugar, and continue beating until the whites form stiff peaks.

Quickly place most of the ice cream on top of the cake (you will have a little extra). Leave at least an inch of cake around the top edge so the ice cream doesn't slide down the sides. Using a spatula, spread the meringue on top of and around the ice cream and cake, making sure no cake or ice cream is visible.

Quickly pop the wooden board into the oven, and leave it there just until the meringue browns lightly, about 4 to 5 minutes. Remove it from the oven, and serve the Baked Hawley at once. Serves 4 to 6 rhubarb fans.

Rhubarb, Rhubarb, Rhubarb!

This elegant cat on the set of the film Rhubarb *was not the title cat, who was scruffier.*

Love, Laughter, and Rhubarb

Bars and Cakes

Rhubarb in Fiction

Rhubarb is more than an ingredient. It can also be a plot point. I have read three novels that highlight rhubarb (actually four: one of the three has a sequel).

I have frequently warned friends, television viewers, and readers not to eat rhubarb leaves, which have high levels of oxalic acid, a poison. In the midst of these warnings I have noted that someone could write a murder mystery in which rhubarb was the weapon. (I admit it: I was toying with the idea myself!)

It turns out that at least two people have already written such mysteries. Rhubarb isn't the ideal weapon for murder. Donald G. Barceloux does write in his *Medical Toxicology of Natural Substances* (Wiley, 2008) that "[c]onsumption of rhubarb leaves as a food substitute for spinach was encouraged in England during World War I until several deaths were attributed to the ingestion of cooked leaves."

Nevertheless, in general it appears that it would take an enormous number of rhubarb leaves to kill the average person, who would surely notice that he or she was being fed them at some point. They don't really look like spinach or any other edible green. (I don't know how they taste—I'm unwilling to risk my health to that extent—but I imagine they don't taste much like spinach, either.)

Consequently, in Lou Jane Temple's mystery *Death by Rhubarb* (St. Martin's Press, 1995), rhubarb is used as a weapon only in a bungled murder attempt. Temple's sleuth, café-owner and caterer Heaven Lee, recognizes the leaves in a salad before they are actually served to anyone. The natural substance successfully used as a poison in this novel is another plant entirely. (I won't spoil the plot by telling you what it is.) The book is clearly misnamed, but I find it hard to blame Temple; she found a great title and decided to stick with it.

Diana Saco conquers the question of rhubarb leaves' strength in *Pushing Up Rhubarb* (Arctic Zebra Press, 2015). In this whodunit, culinary detective Nina Braco discovers that the culprit has distilled rhubarb leaves to increase their potency and then added them to a rhubarb recipe.

Rhubarb almost becomes a character in this novel. Nina describes many people's feelings about the plant when she says to a friend, "A vegetable that you cook like a fruit? A red stalk with poisonous leaves? A tart plant that you have to work hard to make sweet? Everything about rhubarb is just plain wrong.... It looks like celery that's gone red with embarrassment."

Of course, Nina ends up eating her words after sampling a little rhubarb.

My other rhubarb novel is well known. In 1946 Doubleday and Co. published H. Allen Smith's *Rhubarb: The Hilarious Story of a Cat Who Inherited a Baseball Team*. The book's subtitle reveals its major flaw; Smith, a journalist turned humorist, is a little too pleased with how very funny he thinks his book is. Today's reader—this reader, at any rate—may find the book a bit forced, particularly in its portrayal of screwball female characters. Nonetheless, it does offer some truly memorable scenes. And its main character, an ornery cat who is given the name Rhubarb by baseball lovers because he loves a brangle, is fun and believable.

Rhubarb inspired a sequel, *Son of Rhubarb* (Trident Press, 1967). Like all cats, Rhubarb eventually meets his maker. His baseball-team ownership has led to great things; he is the world's richest cat at the time of his death. The inevitable question of finding an heir arises. This tale is even slighter than its predecessor, and its humor is even more suspect. It can boast of a few fine moments, however, including passages in which characters debate whether kittens can be considered legitimate offspring of their sires. It turns out that they can … but perhaps only in Puerto Rico. (You'll have to read the book to follow the logic of this decision.)

The original *Rhubarb* was made into a film in 1951, released by Paramount Pictures. This version of the story, which starred Ray Milland, managed to tone down some of the more risqué and strange elements of the novel to produce a rather charming comedy. The American Film Institute *Catalogue of Feature Films* online reports:

According to news items and studio publicity material, contained in the file on the film at the AMPAS Library, producers William Perlberg and George Seaton spent six months searching for a cat to play Rhubarb and held auditions to find one. Bing Crosby and James Mason reportedly offered their cats for the part. After reviewing hundreds of applications, the producers selected Orangey Murray, a former stray cat from Sherman Oaks. Frank Inn, assistant trainer of Lassie, trained Orangey Murray for the part. According to publicity, Orangey Murray was given his own dressing room and Hollywood apartment, where he lived with his stand-ins during filming.

Turner Classic Movies notes that in the end, counting the stand-ins, a total of 14 cats ended up portraying the film feline. That dressing room must have been pretty chaotic.

Rhubarb the cat was used in advertising as well as film.

Other novels have featured rhubarb in their titles, including Kenneth Allott and Stephen Tait's *The Rhubarb Tree* (The Cresset Press, 1937), involving in part at least "a fascist dystopia" (according to the online database *Utopian Literature in English* by Lyman Tower Sargent); Gaston Bonheur and Pierre Galante's *Moi, Rhubarb* (Gautier-Languerea, 1962), the memoir of a successful cat depicted on the front cover in a business suit; and Stephen Cosgrove's *Rhubarb* (Serendipity, 1995), a children's book about the relationship of a working dog to the other animals on a farm.

Someday I hope to read them all and perhaps write one myself. In the meantime, I will continue making rhubarb bars and cakes. This group of dishes is probably the most likely in this book to tempt non-rhubarb lovers. I have to admit, I'm pretty crazy about these recipes. I was gifted—or cursed, depending on how you look at it—with a sweet tooth.

Rhubarb White Chocolate-Chip Blondies

This recipe is adapted from one I was given by Graham McCulloch, the father of one of my nephew's friends and the general manager of La Prima Catering in Washington, D.C. Graham brought blondies from the company to a party for the kids, and they went like a flash. He was kind enough to share the recipe—and of course I added rhubarb to it! Both the color and the tart flavor of the rhubarb set off the white chocolate nicely.

1/4 pound (1 stick) sweet butter at room temperature
2 cups brown sugar, lightly packed
2 eggs, beaten
2 teaspoons baking powder
3/4 teaspoon salt
2-3/4 cups flour
1 cup white chocolate chips
1 cup finely chopped rhubarb

Grease a 9-by-13-inch pan. Preheat the oven to 325 degrees.

Combine the butter, the brown sugar, and the eggs. Beat until smooth. Beat in the baking powder and the salt. Stir in the flour, followed by the chocolate chips and the rhubarb. The batter will be stiff.

Spoon the batter into the prepared pan. Press it down with the palm of your hand in order to get it to hold together and fill the pan. Bake the blondies until they turn light brown and solidify (25 to 30 minutes).

Cool the blondies in their pan on a wire rack. Cut them into 12 rectangles, and cut each rectangle diagonally into two triangles. Makes 24 triangles.

Jan Carr's Rhubarb Brownies

Dark chocolate, rhubarb, and nuts combine here to make a decadent treat. This recipe comes from Jan Carr of Heath, Massachusetts. I have made it several times and have (so far) been unable to achieve any texture other than "gooey." I don't really mind gooey, however, so I'm still including the recipe here. You may want to keep your brownies in the freezer after slicing them; that's what I do.

1 cup sugar
1/2 cup vegetable or canola oil
2 eggs
1 teaspoon vanilla
1/2 teaspoon baking powder
1/2 teaspoon sea salt
1/2 cup flour
1/3 cup cocoa powder
1 cup diced rhubarb (small pieces)
1/2 cup dark chocolate chips
1/2 cup chopped pecans or walnuts

Preheat the oven to 375 degrees. Line an 8-inch-square pan with parchment paper, and lightly butter the parchment.

In a medium-size bowl whisk together the sugar, the oil, the eggs, and the vanilla. Whisk in the baking powder and the salt.

In another bowl whisk together the flour and the cocoa powder. Stir the wet ingredients into the dry ingredients until they are just incorporated. Stir in the rhubarb, the chocolate chips, and the nuts.

Pour the batter into the prepared pan. Bake the brownies until a toothpick inserted into the center comes out almost clean. Jan says that this takes 20 to 30 minutes, but in my experience the baking time is more like 40 minutes. (Check early and often!) Let the brownies cool for 1/2 hour before cutting them into squares.

Jan says, "Try not to eat them all at once!"

Makes 9 to 25 squares, depending on how big you cut them.

Rhubarb with Cocoa

This second brownie recipe (really, can one have too many brownie recipes?) takes its name from my beloved pets, Rhubarb the cat and Cocoa the dog. They spend a lot of time together quite happily so I wanted to name a recipe after their friendship.

10 tablespoons (1 stick plus 2 tablespoons) sweet butter
1 cup sugar
1/3 cup Dutch-process cocoa
1/2 teaspoon salt
1/2 teaspoon baking powder
1 teaspoon vanilla
2 eggs
1 cup flour
6 ounces (1 cup) chocolate chips
1/4 cup rhubarb jam (see pages 56-57)

Preheat the oven to 350 degrees. Grease an 8-inch-square pan.

In a 2-quart saucepan over low heat, melt the butter. Add the sugar, and stir to combine. Return the mixture to the heat briefly, stirring, until it is hot but not bubbling. (It will start to shine as you stir it.)

Remove it from the heat, and let it cool briefly while you assemble the other ingredients.

Stir in the cocoa, the salt, the baking powder, and the vanilla. Add the eggs, beating until smooth; then stir in the flour and the chocolate chips. Spoon the batter into your pan. Drop little bits of jam on top so that each brownie square will get a small amount; then swirl the jam just a bit.

Bake the brownies until they seem to be starting to solidify, about 30 minutes. Do not over bake. Remove them from the oven. Cool the brownies completely before cutting and serving them. Makes about 16 brownies, depending on how large you cut them.

Buttery Rhubarb Squares

This recipe is adapted from one I had for apple "brownies," originally from Lois Brown of South Deerfield, Massachusetts. It's very moist so the bars are sometimes hard to remove from the pan. They are worth the effort, however.

1/2 cup (1 stick) melted sweet butter
1 cup sugar
2 cups chopped rhubarb
1 egg, beaten
1/2 teaspoon baking soda
1/2 teaspoon baking powder
1/4 teaspoon salt
1 teaspoon ground cinnamon
1 cup flour

Preheat the oven to 350 degrees. Generously grease and flour an 8-inch-square pan.

Stir together the melted butter and the sugar, followed by the rhubarb. Mix in the egg, stirring well to incorporate; then add the baking soda, the baking powder, the salt, and the cinnamon. Stir in the flour, and pour the batter into the prepared pan.

Bake until a toothpick inserted into the center of the bars comes out clean, about 35 to 45 minutes. Makes about 9 to 12 bars, depending on how big you cut them.

Rhubarb Meringue Squares

This rich, delectable recipe comes from my friend Clare Pearson. You may double the recipe and use a 9-by-13-inch pan. If you try that (and there is no reason why you shouldn't), you may have to increase the baking time slightly.

for the crust:
1 cup flour
1 tablespoon sugar
1/2 cup (1 stick) cold sweet butter

for the filling:
2-2/3 tablespoons (2 tablespoons plus 2 teaspoons) flour
1 cup sugar
1/2 teaspoon salt
3 egg yolks, beaten
1/2 cup whipping cream
2-1/2 cups chopped rhubarb (small pieces)

for the meringue:
3 egg whites
1/4 teaspoon cream of tartar
6 tablespoons sugar
1 teaspoon vanilla

Begin with the crust. Preheat the oven to 350 degrees. In a bowl combine the flour and the sugar. Cut in the butter until the mixture is crumbly. Press the crust into the bottom of an 8-inch-square baking pan. Bake for 20 minutes. Cool the crust on a wire rack while you prepare the filling. (Leave the oven on!)

In a bowl combine the flour, the sugar, and the salt for the filling. Stir in the egg yolks and the cream. Add the rhubarb, and pour the filling over the crust. Bake the bars until they are set, at least 45 minutes.

Toward the end of the baking time, start the meringue. In a mixing bowl beat the egg whites and the cream of tartar on medium speed until soft peaks form. Gradually beat in the sugar, 1 tablespoon at a time, until stiff peaks form. Beat in the vanilla.

Spread the meringue over the hot filling. Bake until the meringue has golden-brown highlights (about 12 to 15 minutes). Cool on a wire rack, and cut into squares.

You may refrigerate leftovers, but this dessert is best eaten the first day; the meringue will suffer a little in the refrigerator. Makes 9 to 16 bars, depending on how big you cut them.

Rhubarb Dump Cake

A dump cake, not surprisingly, is assembled by just throwing—that is, dumping—ingredients into a pan. I generally avoid cake mixes. I believe that my standard yellow cake recipe is much healthier and tastier than any box cake. It's also almost as easy to assemble as a mix. I tried making this "cake" (it's actually more like a crisp) from scratch. To my chagrin, using the mix is a lot easier and produces better texture. Just this once, I encourage you to buy a mix.

This recipe came from my friend Vicky Griswold, who works harder than just about anyone I know and still manages to put dinner on the table for her family every evening. If I didn't like Vicky so much, I would resent her energy and competence.

4 cups chopped rhubarb
1/2 cup sugar
1 teaspoon cinnamon
1 package yellow cake mix (16 to 18 ounces, depending on the mix)
1 cup water (or milk, according to cake-mix directions; some mixes require milk)
1/4 cup (1/2 stick) sweet butter, melted

Preheat the oven to 350 degrees. Grease a 9-by-13-inch nonreactive baking dish. Spread the rhubarb evenly in the bottom of the prepared pan. Sprinkle the sugar over the rhubarb, followed by the cinnamon and finally the cake mix. Pour the water (or milk) and the melted butter over the top. Do not stir. Bake for 45 minutes or until the rhubarb is tender.

Serve by itself or with whipped cream, ice cream, or frozen yogurt. Serves 8 to 10.

Strawberry-Rhubarb Shortcake

Rhubarb makes strawberry shortcake even more satisfying. The shortcakes here are based on a recipe from King Arthur Flour. I use either that flour or White Lily brand.

for the filling:
1/2 cup sugar
3 cups chopped rhubarb
the juice of 1/2 lemon

for the self-rising biscuits:
2 cups self-rising flour, plus additional flour as needed for shaping
2 tablespoons sugar
1 cup heavy cream
1 teaspoon vanilla
a small amount of melted butter (optional)
coarse white sugar (optional)

for assembly:
3 cups chopped strawberries
sweetened whipped cream

A couple of hours before you want to begin working, sprinkle the sugar over the rhubarb in a nonreactive saucepan. Stir in the lemon juice, and allow the rhubarb to juice up.

After an hour has passed prepare your filling. (You may make the filling in advance and refrigerate it until it is needed.) Bring the rhubarb mixture to a boil, reduce the heat, and cook, stirring, until the rhubarb becomes thick (about 5 to 7 minutes).

Allow the rhubarb to cool. While it is cooling you may begin making your shortcake biscuits. Preheat the oven to 425 degrees.

Whisk together the flour and the sugar. In a separate bowl (or a measuring cup) combine the cream and the vanilla.

Make a well in the middle of the dry ingredients. Pour the cream and vanilla into the well, and gently stir until the mixture is combined.

Turn the dough onto a floured work surface, and sprinkle a little more flour on top. Fold the dough over several times; then pat it into a circle or rectangle that is about 1/2 inch thick.

Using a sharp biscuit cutter, cut the dough into rounds, about 2 to 2-1/4 inches wide (or however wide you want them!). Place them on an ungreased cookie sheet. (You may line the sheet with parchment or silicone if you're paranoid about sticking, as I am.) If you like, brush the tops of your biscuits with melted butter and sprinkle a little coarse sugar on top.

Bake the biscuits until they are golden brown (12 to 16 minutes).

When you are ready to assemble your shortcakes, cut the biscuits in half horizontally. Spoon the cooked filling onto the bottom halves, followed by the strawberries; then dollop on whipped cream. Top with the biscuit tops. Serves 8.

Deb Porter's Rhubarb Coffee Cake

Deb Porter is a powerhouse at my church in Charlemont, Massachusetts. She spearheads the "pastoral care" committee, which among other things organizes the church's weekly coffee hour. This cake is a coffee-hour favorite.

for the cake:
1-1/4 cups sugar
1 teaspoon baking soda
1/2 teaspoon salt
2 cups flour
2 eggs, beaten
1 cup sour cream
3 cups finely chopped rhubarb

for the topping:
1 cup sugar
1/4 cup (1/2 stick) soft sweet butter
1/4 cup flour
cinnamon as needed

Preheat the oven to 350 degrees. Grease and flour a 9-by-13-inch pan.

In a large bowl stir together the sugar for the cake, the baking soda, the salt, and the flour. Stir in the eggs and the sour cream and combine until smooth; then fold in the rhubarb. Spoon and spread the batter evenly into the prepared pan.

In a small bowl blend the topping ingredients (except the cinnamon) until they are crumbly. Sprinkle those ingredients over the cake, and dust the top with cinnamon.

Bake the cake until a toothpick inserted into the center comes out clean, about 45 minutes. Serves 12 to 16.

Rhubarb Gingerbread

This recipe is adapted from one by a fellow food writer and rhubarb lover. Claire Hopley lives not far from me in Leverett, Massachusetts, although she is English born. Claire writes, "The combination of rhubarb with ginger is one of Mother Nature's perfect pairings." She couldn't be more right. Rhubarb is a tangy surprise in the middle of this spicy cake, which will appeal to anyone with a love of gingerbread.

1/2 cup (1 stick) softened sweet butter
3/4 cup light brown sugar, lightly packed
2 eggs
2 cups flour, divided
3/4 cup molasses and honey (I used half and half) or just molasses
2 teaspoons powdered ginger
1 teaspoon cinnamon
1/2 teaspoon ground cloves
1 teaspoon baking soda
3 tablespoons milk
2 cups chopped rhubarb
confectioner's sugar as needed for dusting

Preheat the oven to 325 degrees. Grease and flour a 10-cup Bundt pan. (You won't use the whole pan, but there is too much batter for a pan half the standard size.)

Cream together the butter and the brown sugar. Beat in the eggs, one at a time, beating in 1 tablespoon of the flour with each one.

Mix in the molasses (and the honey if you're using it) and the spices. When the batter is thoroughly blended, fold in the rest of the flour. Stir the baking soda into the milk until it has dissolved; then gently add it to the gingerbread mixture.

Put half of the batter into the prepared pan. Scatter the rhubarb on top. Spoon in the rest of the batter, making sure that the rhubarb is completely covered.

Bake the cake for 30 minutes; then place a sheet of foil on top. Reduce the heat to 300 degrees, and bake the cake for about 25 minutes more. The cake is done when a toothpick inserted into the top layer of gingerbread comes out clean.

Let the cake cool, and then dust it with confectioner's sugar. Serve warm or at room temperature by itself or with ice cream or whipped cream. Serves 8 to 10.

Rhubarb Jelly-Roll Cake

 One December on my birthday my co-worker Julie Reames introduced me to jelly-roll cake. The cake Julie presented to me was an Alexandria, Virginia, tradition from Shuman's Bakery. Shuman's was founded in 1876 and was a popular source for pastries in town until 2004, when the family members running it retired.

 Six years later, cousins decided to resurrect Shuman's signature dessert, the jelly cake, and sell it online. When Julie unveiled this masterpiece I was stunned. The Shuman cake is wide—15 inches in diameter—and consists of three thin layers of yellow pound cake filled with currant jelly and topped with confectioner's sugar. Mine was gorgeous and tasted light and fresh.

 Of course, I immediately wanted to bake my own jelly-roll cake. Rhubarb lover that I am, I decided to fill MY cake with that tart fruit instead of currants.

 My friend Buckey Grimm mentioned that his mother bakes a similar cake for their family. She graciously supplied her recipe, which I have adapted slightly.

 I didn't want to serve a crowd so I used smaller pans—thin layer-cake pans (about nine inches in diameter) I purchased at Williams-Sonoma. Wilton also sells eight-inch layer pans; if you use these, you might either make another layer or bake the cakes slightly longer.

 With very thin cakes like these it is particularly important to grease and flour the pans thoroughly—a little cut-out parchment (also greased and floured) wouldn't go amiss to help the cakes come out of the pans—and to avoid overcooking the batter.

1/2 cup sweet butter at room temperature
1 cup sugar
1 egg
1 scant teaspoon baking powder
1/2 teaspoon salt
3/4 teaspoon lemon juice
1-1/3 cups flour
1/2 cup milk
3/4 cup rhubarb jam (see page 57), pulverized with an immersion blender to remove any lumps, OR rhubarb curd (see page 58)
confectioner's sugar as needed for dusting

Preheat the oven to 350 degrees. Grease and flour 3 thin layer-cake pans. If you can, cut pieces of parchment to match the bottoms of the pans, place them in the pans, and grease and flour the parchment as well.

In a medium bowl cream the butter; then cream in the sugar. Beat in the egg, followed by the baking powder, the salt, and the lemon juice.

Alternate stirring in the flour and the milk, beginning and ending with the flour.

Divide the batter into the prepared pans and smooth it across the bottoms.

Bake the layers for 12 to 15 minutes, until the cakes have browned a bit and spring back when touched with a finger. Be vigilant to avoid overbaking.

Remove the pans from the oven, and place them on a rack. As soon as you can handle the pans, gently ease out the cakes. Allow them to cool thoroughly on racks.

When the cakes are cool assemble the three layers, spreading jam between the layers but not on top. Dust the top with confectioner's sugar. Serves 6 to 8.

Rhubarb Upside-Down Cake

Sometimes I find it hard to recognize my childhood memories as being about the real me. Of course, I have no trouble recalling the loquaciousness, the adorability, and (I admit it!) the mule-like stubbornness of the young Tinky. But it's hard to believe that I spent my earliest years disliking some of the foods I now adore. I thought spinach was bitter and ugly. I disliked Chinese food so much that when my parents wanted to teach me to eat with chopsticks they fed me ravioli. (By the way, ravioli are a lot harder to pick up with chopsticks than most Chinese food.) And, as I mentioned earlier, I was determined not to eat rhubarb in any form. Today I'm thrilled to see fresh spinach at a farm stand. I long for Chinese food regularly. And rhubarb is probably my favorite fruit. I know. It's not really a fruit. But we treat it as one. It's beautiful. It's resilient. It's versatile. Oh, my goodness. I just realized that I may love rhubarb because it's like ME!

One childhood passion I still retain is a love for upside-down cake. I adapted this recipe from my mother's classic pineapple version.

for the topping (which goes on the bottom!):
1/4 cup (1/2 stick) sweet butter
3/4 cup brown sugar, firmly packed
2 cups rhubarb (1/2-inch chunks)

for the cake:
1/2 cup (1 stick) sweet butter, at room temperature
1 cup sugar
2 eggs
1 tablespoon baking powder
1/4 teaspoon salt
1-3/4 cups flour
1/2 cup milk
2 teaspoons vanilla

Preheat the oven to 350 degrees. Make the topping. Melt the butter in a saucepan. (If you're going to use a cast-iron skillet for baking, use that to melt the butter.)

Stir in the brown sugar and cook, stirring, until it melts and bubbles. Spread the brown-sugar mixture in a 9-inch-square pan or a 10-inch cast-iron skillet. Arrange the rhubarb on top. For the cake, cream together the butter and the sugar. Beat in the eggs, 1 at a time. Add the baking powder and the salt. Stir in the flour alternately with the milk. Stir in the vanilla, and pour the batter over the rhubarb.

Bake the cake until a toothpick inserted into the center comes out clean, about 40 minutes. (If the cake is brown before this happens, decrease the oven temperature.) Allow the cake to cool for 5 to 10 minutes. Loosen the edges with a knife, and invert the cake onto a serving plate held over the baking pan. Turn upside-down. Remove the pan. Serve alone or with whipped cream. Serves 9.

Rhubarb Pound Cake

Few cakes are as satisfying as a buttery pound cake. This simple, rich Bundt works well for breakfast, lunch, dinner, or a snack.

1 cup (2 sticks) sweet butter, at room temperature
2 cups sugar
4 eggs
1 teaspoon vanilla
1 to 3 tablespoons grated orange zest
1 teaspoon baking powder
1/2 teaspoon salt
2 cups chopped rhubarb (in 1/2-inch pieces), plus a bit more if you like
2 tablespoons confectioner's sugar
3 cups flour
more confectioner's sugar as needed for dusting

Preheat the oven to 325 degrees. Grease and flour a 10-inch Bundt pan.

Using an electric mixer, cream the butter until it is fluffy. Beat in the sugar. Beat in the eggs, followed by the vanilla and the zest. Beat in the baking powder and the salt. In a bowl toss the rhubarb in the 2 tablespoons of confectioner's sugar. If the rhubarb still looks wet, coat it with a little of the flour.

On low speed, blend the remaining flour into the butter mixture. Gently fold the rhubarb into the batter. Transfer the batter to the prepared pan. Bake the cake until a toothpick inserted into the center comes out clean, about 1-1/4 hours. If the top seems to be browning too fast but the cake isn't done after 1 hour, reduce the heat to 300 degrees.

Set the pan on a wire rack to cool for 20 minutes; then turn the cake out onto the rack and let it cool completely. When the cake is cool dust it with confectioner's sugar.

Serves 10 to 12.

This 1909 Thanksgiving card got rhubarb's season all wrong!

Odds and Ends

Acknowledgments

Many books are solitary endeavors. Cookbooks tend to be communal efforts. That suits me just fine. I live in a vibrant community of cooks and eaters and see my work as part of an ongoing dialogue with my neighbors.

I thank Lee Peters for this book's wonderful cover and Peter Beck for several of the photographs, including the cover images. (The rest of the photographs are my own, for better or for worse, supplemented by images in the public domain.) Lee and Peter are my heroes, and I applaud their talent and generosity.

I offer thanks to everyone who has provided rhubarb for my recipe testing over the years: Florette Zuelke, Peter Beck, Ken Bertsch, Dennis Anderson, Leslie Clark, the Purdys, Pen and Plow Farm, the Coopers, the Riches, and Wilder Brook Farm. If I have left your name out, please don't be offended!

Thanks as well to my many recipe testers, primarily my family and my neighbors: Alice Parker, Lisa Smart, Peter Beck, Ruth and Duncan Gillan, Esther Haskell, the Federated Church Book Group, Susan and Peter Purdy, Betsy Kovacs, Jack Estes, Lisa Johnson, Will Cosby, Alison Seaton, the Smith Family, and more.

My rhubarb recipes have also found a home over the years with my friends at WWLP-TV/*Mass Appeal*: Seth Stutman, Ashley Kohl, Lauren Zenzie, Danny New, Michelle Stevens, Lisa Lamontagne, Denise Koczocik, and the rest of the crew. Thanks for the support and the camaraderie.

I appreciate the careful proofreading of Peter Beck, Susan Purdy, Lisa Smart, and Leigh Bullard Weisblat. Above all, I want to thank my family: David, Leigh, and Michael. You have housed me, fed me, tasted my concoctions, and supported me. You have even welcomed my sweet but pesky pets into your home.

This book was supported in part by a grant from the Charlemont-Hawley Cultural Council, a local agency which is supported by the Massachusetts Cultural Council, a state agency.

A Note About Cooking with Rhubarb

Remember that rhubarb is acidic. I tried to mention this frequently throughout the recipes, but in case I missed some entries, please remember that rhubarb should be cooked in nonreactive cookware (stainless steel, enamel, glass). Substances like aluminum or copper can alter the color and taste of the rhubarb and be altered themselves in return.

Afterword: Gather Ye Rhubarb While Ye May

I have a love/hate relationship with the idea of food coming from far away. I believe in local produce, but I'm not exclusively a locavore. I don't intend to deprive myself of fruits and vegetables during the winter. Our growing season is short in western Massachusetts, and even foods that store well—squash, potatoes, root vegetables, apples—begin to look wan after a while.

As a salad lover, then, I'm thrilled that I can now get good lettuce year round in most grocery stores, thanks to refrigerator trucks. I also enjoy purchasing artichokes from far away, as well as citrus fruits, which never grow near me but survive the trip north from Florida or Texas quite nicely in the dead of winter.

Some foods don't seem to thrive on travel, and I don't eat them out of season. In my opinion, the colorless tomatoes one sees in grocery stores everywhere during the winter are simply not worth buying. I wait for fresh-tomato season and then eat tomatoes every day. (I also freeze tomato sauce and can salsa when I am able.)

Similarly, once a person gets used to eating corn that was picked only a few hours earlier, it's very hard for her to get excited about the dry, elderly ears that appear in produce bins out of season.

Of course, there exist a very few foods that simply aren't available in grocery stores when they're not in season. The cranberry is one. I start calling stores in the middle of September to find out whether cranberries have appeared. Once they're on the shelves, I go crazy for cranberries. Rhubarb shares this "get it while you can" quality with cranberries. Stores simply don't stock it when it's not in season.

Even frozen rhubarb can be hard to find. Walmart's website says that Dole frozen rhubarb is available in Walmart stores (although not online). I have yet to find a Walmart that stocks it, however.

I have purchased high-quality frozen rhubarb via mail order from Frank Farms, a producer in southwestern Michigan. Ordering frozen rhubarb in this way is expensive—particularly if one is used to having rhubarb appear in one's own yard (or one's neighbors' yards) free of charge. Rhubarb must be shipped overnight, and the shipping can cost as much as, or more than, the actual rhubarb. Nevertheless, the rhubarb is beautifully frozen, and a five-pound bag lasts me a while.

In order to save money, I try to freeze rhubarb myself each spring so that I can satisfy winter cravings without breaking the bank. Somehow or other, however, my frozen rhubarb never lasts through the winter.

In general, I bide my time and wait for rhubarb to shoot out of the ground in May. I enjoy it while I have it—just as I enjoy the sunshine, the daffodils, the green grass, the autumn leaves, and New England's other seasonal joys.

Eating this way, I feel as though I'm channeling my grandmother, who grew up on a farm in Vermont. She had a knack for embracing the seasons when they came along and saying farewell to them without tears when they moved on, confident that she had made the most of her time.

There's a lesson here. Rhubarb and my grandmother remind me always to find joy in the moment. The past is unalterable. The future is unknowable. I can always savor the present, however. And I do.

To the Eaters, Make Much of Time
(with apologies to Richard Herrick)

Gather ye rhubarb while ye may,
While spring is happy hearted.
The rhubarb cobbler we eat today
Soon will have departed.

Recipe Index

Appetizers
    Rhubarb-Glazed Meatballs 45
    Rhubarb and Bacon Compote/Compost 25
    Rhubarb Pizza 46
    Rhubarb Salsa 24
Asparagus Fritters, Tinky's 66
Asparagus Penne, Taffy's 65
Asparagus Risotto with Rhubarb 31
Aunt Lura's Rhubarb Chutney 51

Baked Alaska with Rhubarb Ice Cream 92
Baked Hawley 92
Barbecue Sauce, Tangy Rhubarb 53
Beverages
    Rhubarb Bitters 16
    Rhubarb Cordial 23
    Rhubarb Lemonade 20
    Rhubarb Manhattan 18
    Rhubarb Syrup 20
    Rhubarb Tea 21
    Strawberry-Rhubarb Daiquiri 19
    The Madame Rhubarb 18
Bitters, Rhubarb 16
Blondies, Rhubarb White Chocolate-Chip 98
Bread, Rhubarb 37
Breads, Muffins, and Scones
    Rhubarb Bread 37
    Rhubarb Scones 35
    Rhubarb Sugar-Top Muffins 38
    Susan Purdy's Healthy and Delicious
        Rhubarb Muffins 39
Brownies, Jan Carr's Rhubarb 99
Brownies, Rhubarb with Cocoa 100

Brownies and Bars
    Buttery Rhubarb Squares 101
    Jan Carr's Rhubarb Brownies 99
    Rhubarb Meringue Squares 102
    Rhubarb White Chocolate-Chip Blondies 98
    Rhubarb with Cocoa 100
Buttery Rhubarb Squares 101

Cakes
    Baked Hawley 92
    Deb Porter's Rhubarb Coffee Cake 106
    Rhubarb Dump Cake 103
    Rhubarb Gingerbread 107
    Rhubarb Jelly-Roll Cake 108
    Rhubarb Pound Cake 111
    Rhubarb Upside-Down Cake 110
    Strawberry-Rhubarb Shortcake 104
Catch Up or Catsup or Ketchup, Rhubarb 55
Chantilly, Rhubarb 85
Chicken, Persian Rhubarb Stew with 43
Chili, First-Prize Rhubarb 44
Chipotle Sauce, Rhubarb 59
Chutney, Aunt Lura's Rhubarb 51
Chutney, Toni's Spicy Rhubarb 52
Cobbler, Susan Shauger's Rhubarb 87
Cocktails and Mixers
    Rhubarb Bitters 16
    Rhubarb Cordial 23
    Rhubarb Manhattan 18
    Rhubarb Syrup 20
    Strawberry-Rhubarb Daiquiri 19
    The Madame Rhubarb 18
Coconut-Rhubarb Pie 73
Coffee Cake, Deb Porter's Rhubarb 106
Coleslaw, Stump Sprouts Maple-Rhubarb 34
Compote/Compost, Rhubarb and Bacon 25

Condiments
  Aunt Lura's Rhubarb Chutney 51
  Paula's Raspberry-Rhubarb Jam 56
  Rhubarb and Bacon Compost/Compote 25
  Rhubarb Catch Up or Catsup or Ketchup 55
  Rhubarb Chipotle Sauce 59
  Rhubarb Curd 58
  Rhubarb Salsa 24
  Stewed Rhubarb 83
  Tangy Rhubarb Barbecue Sauce 53
  Tinky's Rhubarb Jam 57
  Toni's Spicy Rhubarb Chutney 52
Cordial, Rhubarb 23
Crisp, Rhubarb-Apple 86
Crumble, Miss Ginny's Rhubarb 88
Curd, Rhubarb 58

Daiquiri, Strawberry-Rhubarb 19
Dandelion-Green Salad 64
Dandelion Greens, Sautéed 63
Deb Porter's Rhubarb Coffee Cake 106
Dump Cake, Rhubarb 103

First-Prize Rhubarb Chili 44
Fritters, Tinky's Asparagus 66

Gingerbread, Rhubarb 107
Grilled Rhubarb 30
Grilled Rhubarb, About 29

Ice Cream, Rhubarb 92

Jams
  Paula's Raspberry-Rhubarb Jam 56
  Tinky's Rhubarb Jam 57
Jan Carr's Rhubarb Brownies 99
Jelly-Roll Cake, Rhubarb 108

Ketchup or Catch Up or Catsup, Rhubarb 55

Lamb and Rhubarb Stew, Persian 48
Lemonade, Rhubarb 20

Madame Rhubarb, The 18
Main Dishes
  First-Prize Rhubarb Chili 44
  Persian Lamb and Rhubarb Stew 48
  Persian Rhubarb Stew with Chicken 43
  Rhubarb-Glazed Meatballs 45
  Rhubarb Pizza 46
  Swordfish Steak with Rhubarb Salsa 50
  Taffy's Asparagus Penne 65
Manhattan, Rhubarb 18
Meatballs, Rhubarb-Glazed 45
Miss Ginny's Rhubarb Crumble 88
Mom's Rhubarb Pie 75
Muffins, Rhubarb Sugar-Top 38
Muffins, Susan Purdy's Healthy and Delicious
    Rhubarb 39

Nantucket Rhubarb Pie 77

Paula's Raspberry-Rhubarb Jam 56
Penne, Taffy's Asparagus 65
Persian Lamb and Rhubarb Stew 48
Persian Rhubarb Stew with Chicken 43
Picking Rhubarb 22
Pies and Tarts
  Coconut-Rhubarb Pie 73
  Mom's Rhubarb Pie 75
  Nantucket Rhubarb Pie 77
  Rustic Rhubarb Tart 76
  Strawberry-Rhubarb Cream-Cheese Tart 78
Pie Crust
  About 71
  Basic Shortening Pie Crust 72
Pizza, Rhubarb 46
Pound Cake, Rhubarb 111

Raspberry-Rhubarb Jam, Paula's 56
Rhubarb-Apple Crisp 86
Rhubarb and Bacon Compost/Compote 25
Rhubarb Barbecue Sauce, Tangy 53
Rhubarb Bitters 16

Rhubarb Bread 37
Rhubarb Brownies 99-100
Rhubarb Catsup or Catch Up or Ketchup 55
Rhubarb Chantilly 85
Rhubarb Chili, First-Prize 44
Rhubarb Chipotle Sauce 59
Rhubarb Chutney, Aunt Lura's 51
Rhubarb Chutney, Toni's Spicy 52
Rhubarb Cobbler, Susan Shauger's 87
Rhubarb Coffee Cake, Deb Porter's 106
Rhubarb Cordial 23
Rhubarb Crumble, Miss Ginny's 88
Rhubarb Curd 58
Rhubarb Dump Cake 103
Rhubarb Gingerbread 107
Rhubarb-Glazed Meatballs 45
Rhubarb, Grilled 30
Rhubarb Jam, Tinky's 57
Rhubarb Jelly-Roll Cake 108
Rhubarb Lemonade 20
Rhubarb Meringue Squares 102
Rhubarb Muffins, Susan Purdy's 39
Rhubarb Pizza 46
Rhubarb Pound Cake 111
Rhubarb Salsa 24
Rhubarb Scones 35
Rhubarb Sorbet 89
Rhubarb Sugar-Top Muffins 38
Rhubarb Syrup 20
Rhubarb Tea 21
Rhubarb Upside-Down Cake 110
Rhubarb White Chocolate-Chip Blondies 98
Rhubarb with Cocoa Brownies 100
Risotto, Asparagus with Rhubarb 31
Rustic Rhubarb Tart 76

Salads
  Sort of Grad's Father's Dandelion Salad 64
  Strawberry-Rhubarb Spinach Salad 32
  Stump-Sprouts Maple-Rhubarb Coleslaw 34

Salsa, Rhubarb 24
Sauce, Rhubarb Chipotle 59
Sautéed Dandelion Greens 63
Scones, Rhubarb 35
Shortcake, Strawberry-Rhubarb 104
Side Dishes
  Asparagus Risotto with Rhubarb 31
  Grilled Rhubarb 30
  Sautéed Dandelion Greens 63
  Taffy's Asparagus Penne 65
  Tinky's Asparagus Fritters 66
Sorbet, Rhubarb 89
Sort of Grad's Father's Dandelion Salad 64
Stew, Persian Lamb and Rhubarb 48
Stew, Persian Rhubarb with Chicken 43
Stewed Rhubarb 83
Strawberry-Rhubarb Cream-Cheese Tart 78
Strawberry-Rhubarb Daiquiri 19
Strawberry-Rhubarb Shortcake 104
Strawberry-Rhubarb Spinach Salad 32
Strawberry-Rhubarb Trifle 84
Stump Sprouts Maple-Rhubarb Coleslaw 34
Susan Purdy's Healthy and Delicious Rhubarb
    Muffins 39
Susan Shauger's Rhubarb Cobbler 87
Swordfish Steak with Rhubarb Salsa 50
Syrup, Rhubarb 20

Taffy's Asparagus Penne 65
Tangy Rhubarb Barbecue Sauce 53
Tart, Rustic Rhubarb 76
Tart, Strawberry-Rhubarb Cream-Cheese 78
Tea, Rhubarb 21
Tinky's Asparagus Fritters 66
Tinky's Rhubarb Jam 57
Toni's Spicy Rhubarb Chutney 52
Trifle, Strawberry-Rhubarb 84

Upside-Down Cake, Rhubarb 110